God Has Better Things to do Than My Laundry (and Other Observations From an Overly Dramatic Mom)

By Heather Nestleroad

Copyright 2012 Heather Nestleroad

Print ISBN # 978-0-9860059-1-6

Second edition - January 2013

Edited and published by PublishSavvy

Cover art by Karen Nowosatko

All Bible quotes/scripture are from the *Life Application Study Bible, New International Version*, 1991.

All rights reserved. This book may not be reproduced in any form, in whole or in part, without written permission from the author.

Table of Contents

Dedication

Introduction

Chapter 1: Focus

Chapter 2: Love & Marriage: Pillow Talk

Chapter 3: Stay at Home Mom Tribulations: Who's the Boss?

Chapter 4: Teenagers: The Reason God Gave us Pharmacies

Chapter 5: The Aunt Flo Follies: Who REALLY Pays the "Monthly Bill"?

Chapter 6: Not So-Hollywood Holidays

Chapter 7: Don't Ask Me – I Just Live Here

Chapter 8: Neurotic Much?

Chapter 9: Ya Gotta Have Friends – and Chocolate

Chapter 10: Pretty Food Lovers, Unite

Chapter 11: Fitness Fool, or Foolishly Not Fit?

Chapter 12: It Takes a Village ... and a Lot of Time

Chapter 13: I Gotta Go Back, Back, Back to Work Again

Chapter 14: Goin' For Broke

Chapter 15: Random Observations

Chapter 16: Keepin' The Faith, But Not Like Billy Joel

Chapter 17: Keeping it Real... Serious

Chapter 18: Conversations Only a Mother Could Love

Chapter 19: I Want to Grow Up, I Want to Grow Old, I Want to Grow Wings

Chapter 20: Roses are Red (poems)

Acknowledgements

About the Author

Dedication*

For my perfect little angels, "Daphne," "Megan," and "Scotty": I love you to the moon and back and everywhere in between.

For my sweetheart, "Vaughn": You complete me.

All names have been changed to protect the not-so-innocent, innocents.

Introduction

Before you invest any time into this book, you should be warned about what you're in for. So here are some neurotic things about me you should know.

I am a terrible mother. I expect my kids to make their beds, bring their dirty laundry down to be washed, clean up their space at the table, shower and brush their teeth daily, and eat vegetables. And, there's more.

I won't let them watch a PG13 movie unless I have previewed it first, lights out by 9 P.M., no one is allowed outside after dark, there is no foul language, no pushing, no hitting, no slamming of doors (now impossible since I removed the door handles), and if you can't get along, I make you hold hands and say at least five nice things about each other. I have also been known to tie their hands together and make them help each other eat (and other daily things) so they can learn to rely on each other.

I have taken away all electronic screens for weeks, and I have also told them about the pain of having children. The girls know that boys have cooties and the boy knows that girls have cooties and they don't get rid of them until after college when cooties die from old age, so having a boyfriend or girlfriend is off limits. Perhaps you think this is going too far.

I want them to be able to hire someone to cook for them, or to eat out a lot, because I cannot teach them to cook. It's difficult because every time they walk in to see what is for dinner, they get grossed out over raw meat.

I can teach them to order good food from a restaurant, respect each other and themselves, and everyone they come in contact with. I also plan to teach them to be afraid of the dark so they won't try to sneak out of the house when they are older.

When I was pregnant with my first child, I used to drink milk and root beer out of the containers and swish them around together in my mouth. That way I could have a root beer float at any time during the day. I'm not allowed to do that anymore. Those were good times.

I refuse to go to bed until a show/movie is over. It doesn't matter if I've seen it, own it on DVD, or have it recorded on the DVR, or if I'm recording it as I watch it. I have to see the end. I'm not sure if this means: A) I think it will end differently, B) I think the end is best, C) I like to see things through to the end, or D) I'm nuts.

I call Kings Island Amusement Park "the island of kings" because I think it sounds more exotic and fun. I only go to Kings Island for the blue ice cream. I only go to Disney because I love Mickey Mouse, I want to relive the childhood I wish I had had, and for the buffet at Hollywood and Vine. What can I say? I'm very food-oriented. I eat "spaghetti" ice cream from the local ice cream place because A) My daughter thinks it's disgusting to eat something called spaghetti ice cream, even though she hasn't tried it. B) It has strawberries in it and as we all know, if ice cream has fruit in it, it can't be that fattening. C) It is my job to drive my children nuts.

I enjoy singing in the car while I'm driving alone. I enjoy this very much because no one is around to tell me to "stop singing—the coyotes are starting to howl." Sometimes I do this with the kids in the car as a punishment.

My idea of a mixed drink is an Orange Julius. My idea of the perfect candy is peanut M&Ms. My idea of a perfect meal is one I didn't cook. My idea of a delicacy is when we splurge for the "good cheese" that isn't Kraft slices. My idea of a good time is sock skating on my wood floors while singing to the iPod. My idea of a perfect invention is laundry that folds itself.

When I eat out, I like to order ice water with lemon, or tea with lemon. Not because I like the flavor of the lemon in my drink, but because I think it makes the glass look pretty.

The size-8 me and the size-6 me recently ganged up on the size-4 me and kicked my hiney. Swimsuit season is on its way and I no longer will need a life preserver, as I now have one built in. I have a dream of flying, and the flaps on my upper arms may just be big enough now to make that a reality.

My children told me to invest in that cream that takes away stretch marks. My husband says no new flip-flops unless I paint my toenails.

If I could just get to menopause, I could turn my frozen fingers and toes into toasty phalanges.

I have woken myself up with a snort before, but I don't think I snore. Also, I don't dream. At least, not that I remember. Unless you count the dream I had after Michael Jackson died. I had a dream that we were pals and he came over to visit. He'd brought me his entire collection to give to my daughter as a gift. Also I think I may have had a dream once where I passed out attempting Zumba, and got trampled by a bunch of sweaty ladies. I can't be sure though.

So, you see, I'm really easy to get along with.

Focus

I am lacking focus. I might have ADD. I might be lazy. I might just be out of it. I'm not sure what the trouble is. Maybe I need new glasses. Maybe I need to stay off Facebook and Pinterest. (OK, I really need to stay off those. They are a colossal waste of time.) Maybe I should exercise. That could help with my focus.

The other day I was watching an Ellen DeGeneres stand-up, where she says she thinks she has ADD. She is assured of this because she doesn't even have the patience to take a test to see if she has ADD.

I once told my grandmother that I was having trouble with forgetting things, and that I could use some ginkgo. So she ordered me some. The problem is that I needed something or someone to remind me to take the ginkgo, so I could remember all the other stuff I was forgetting. I eventually took them all. I think there was a 30-day supply; it may have taken me six months or 60 days. Who remembers? Then, I was watching Ellen again, and she said if you can remember the ginkgo, you probably don't need the ginkgo. So I felt good, because it's not just me.

I enjoy watching Ellen's stand-up comedy because she talks about so much that I wonder about. Why do they package batteries like they do, and only put light bulbs in the flimsy cardboard? I have asked myself the same thing.

I wonder about other things too. Why do people complain when we have 60-degree weather in January? Isn't that the most fantastic thing ever?

Does pork ever think that chicken is the other white meat?

The washer is only putting out hot water. The dryer is only drying on hot.

If brussels sprouts are so good for you, why don't they taste like chocolate, or at least like carrots?

Why isn't a Reese's Cup a health food, if chocolate has milk, which does the body good, and peanut butter has protein?

Does Lady Gaga scare everyone else, or is it just me?

My DVR is filling up with unwatched shows.

I'm afraid to fall, from any height.

How do cows stay warm in the winter? I had a leather coat once and it was not warm.

How do the people from Classmates.com find you, and why don't they get if you wanted to keep in touch, you would have?

How do people get to that place as an adult where running is fun?

Would my mother have kept drinking her coffee black if she knew about chocolate creamer? She was the ultimate junk food junkie. I can see that taking her love of coffee and chocolate to a whole new level.

The yard needs to be mowed. Again.

Do other people go into the garage, sit in their car, plug in the iPod, and sing at the top of their lungs, to feel like a rock star?

If I had been a dog, I would have been Doug from the movie "UP." Squirrel! If I had been able to learn everything to the tune of a song, I might have been a rocket scientist... OK, that's not true. I never wanted to be a rocket scientist. In fact, I have never known or known anyone who aspired to be a rocket scientist. I might have become a doctor or nurse. Well, probably not, because I don't do well with vomit. I actually don't know what I would have been. I cannot think of a single thing that seems so interesting that I wouldn't get distracted at some point.

My best friend knew at age seven that she would become a teacher. When I was six, I wanted to be a teacher; by the time I was eight, I wanted to be a hairdresser. When I was ten, I wanted to be a ballerina; by the time I was seventeen, I wanted to be a fashion designer. This may be why I love reading so much. I can be anything in a book. Then I can pick up a different book and be something else.

So back to the focus issue. I have laundry to do. I need to go get a mocha, because I haven't hit my quota for the day. I need to walk aimlessly through the house so I can say I exercised today. I need to use the restroom ....

OK, I'm back. What was I saying? Oh yes, focus.

Don't ask me to read all the instructions to cook dinner, because that won't happen. I won't cover the dish when I'm supposed to, and I will cover it when I am not supposed to. I will leave something out.

Don't ask me to drive you anywhere further than 20 minutes away, because I will get bored and start singing, or ask you to drive so I can read.

Any deadline you may have for me better be a ruse. It might be best to tell me one day, hoping that I get it to you three days later. Because focus seems to be an issue for me.

Love and Marriage: Pillow Talk

Vaughn: Do you know four score and seven years ago?

Heather: Uh, yeah, Abe Lincoln right?

Vaughn: Yes, but do you know how long a score is?

Heather: Is that a musical thing? It's 11:30, and I'm tired, so can you just tell me?

Vaughn: It's 20 years, honey.

Heather: <finally realizing what he's saying> Oh crap, today is the 14th, isn't it? I'm sorry. Happy anniversary.

Yesterday was the 20th anniversary of the day my husband and I met. We have been together since that day, and although we don't necessarily celebrate the day, he always remembers.

This could be a good thing or a bad thing. Good because he loves me and wants to celebrate, or bad because it's the day he realizes perhaps he should have stayed home and not walked across the yard to come meet me in the first place. I'm certainly glad he did.

Before children, when I used to look at a calendar and know what the date was, I knew what was going on. I was a reasonably intelligent human being. However, three kids later, I realize I have no idea what the date is on any given day.

I once forgot my best friend's birthday. I even had a one-hour conversation with her that day. All during that call, it didn't once occur to me to tell her happy birthday. And she let me go on, until the next day, when she called me, and said "Are you going to tell me happy birthday or are we just not celebrating this year?" This, roughly translated in Christi-speak, means "Hey loser, yesterday was my birthday. Tell me happy birthday before I think you don't care anymore. Oh and by the way, now you owe me two lunches!"

I think this is what happens when you are comfortable in your life. I know that certain dates hold special meanings; I just don't know what the date is. So, it's not that I necessarily forgot, per se. I am just too comfortable in my surroundings, and so thankful every day, that it doesn't occur to me that another day is more special than the last. Now May 6th (our wedding anniversary) I remember, and although he always remembers January 14th, I usually just look forward to May.

The Pharmacist's Wife

I am married to a drug dealer.

Now that I have your attention, what I meant to say is, I am married to a pharmacist. I would like to further clarify that I am only MARRIED to a pharmacist, and as such, have no training whatsoever about drugs in general. I have no idea which cough syrup is the best for your condition, and I wouldn't know a blood pressure pill from Viagra by sight.

For whatever reason, I am the one who gets questions about medication, like I've learned all that my husband knows simply by living in the same house with him for many years. In fact, when I go to the doctor, they know what my husband does too, so usually, they ask me which medication I want to be on. I honestly don't know the difference between an Advil and a Tylenol, other than the fact that they are different colors.

My husband graduated from Purdue University after five years; his was the last class to do it in five, as now they go for six years. When we were in college, I would help him study. He would have to name pills on sight and draw chemical structures. He is really brilliant.

Now, to answer the FAQs.

1. No, we do not have all kinds of "good" drugs at our house.

2. There are other benefits from his job. Because he is a retail pharmacist, I am now spoiled in ways you wouldn't necessarily expect. I rarely buy milk. He also brings home tea, laundry detergent, fabric softener, Advil, office supplies, shampoo, body wash, dishwasher detergent, and I'm sure a slew of things I'm forgetting. (On the other hand, I have to go buy Midol myself, because he doesn't think it's necessary. There are three women of child-bearing age in the house. I say it's necessary.)

3. We also do not go to the doctor until our (his) best efforts (i.e., over-the-counter meds) have been exhausted.

4. This year, I had to get my first flu shot because he had to learn how to do it. It would have looked bad if I didn't trust him to practice on me. I will say that he was very good and I barely felt a thing.

5. I do have an associate's degree in Medical Assisting, and, with three kids, I do know a bit about injuries. He, however, does not handle blood well. Other illnesses he handles like a trooper; thankfully, if vomit is involved, he usually cleans it up.

So, I guess the moral of the story is this: if it's advice on drugs you want, I cannot help you. I am only married to a pharmacist. Any questions you have on medications, or the weird rash you have, or if you feel like you're going to throw up, ask him. I will even give you his work number.

If you're bleeding, come to me. And the person you ask if you are looking for a good pharmacist is me, because I married the best one.

How Deep Is Your Love?

It does not escape my notice that I have been very blessed indeed. My husband and I have been married for almost sixteen years. We have been together for twenty-one. We met our senior year in high school.

I was this skinny girl, with the typical big eighties hair. I went to school, and then went to work at the mall. I spent my entire check on 1) clothes at the "cool" store in the mall and 2) gas to get to work so I could earn more money to buy clothes. I was neither too pretty nor too ugly, and I was far from popular. I also had the worst self-esteem, which I'm trying to this day to outgrow.

He was this cute, brown-haired, puppy-dog-brown-eyed guy. He was neither too tall nor too short. He was just the right height for a short girl like me and those eyes were nothing short of dreamy. (They still are.) I remember the night we met as clearly as if it were yesterday.

I was friends with his next-door neighbor, and she was dating a friend of his. They invited us over on the same night. He almost didn't show up. To this day, I have no idea where her parents were. We sat around in awkward silence, drinking Coke and playing with these little pink plastic bugs that would jump whenever you pushed on their bottoms.

My friend and her boyfriend left to go pick up a pizza, leaving us there alone to talk. We talked, and I always say when he flipped the pink plastic bug into my Coke, I knew. I waited days for him to call me and ask me out. He eventually did. Even when he spilled water on me, and I sang in the car to "Janie's Got a Gun," neither one of us was scared off.

I remember the first kiss. It was the first kiss that ever took my breath away. The kind you feel all the way down to your toes. Our first Valentine's Day together, he was taking a class at the local college. The snow was accumulating, and yet he didn't go home after class. He trekked to my house to bring me flowers, candy, and a card. My mother loved him. (I have always said, and still believe to this day, that she would have traded me for him, any day of the week and twice on Sunday.)

He used to write me poems and love letters. When we were in college, they came in the mail regularly. We would write of our hopes and our dreams, and how one day we would get married, and the waiting would be worth it.

It was. We were together five years before we married.

Finishing college was the best decision we made. After all these years, we realize that every day is a gift. We know that each day — not just Valentine's Day — is cause for celebration. We were in the store last week and picked out cards for each other. We read them, and then put them back on the shelf. We used the card money to buy a drink in the checkout line instead.

I've had the big gesture. Actually, I'm living the big gesture. I'm married to the most amazing husband and father. If I knew nothing else, other than the fact that he would one day become the father to our children, it would have been enough.

Isn't that how true love works, after all? My Heavenly Father reminds me daily that with great sacrifice comes great reward. I still have every letter and poem from those early years. I even have the pink plastic bug that he flipped into my Coke.

Those were the beginnings of our love; the greatest gesture, however, is in the sticking it out, arm in arm, up the hills and down the valleys of life, that makes me respond to the song "How deep is your love?" with another song: "There ain't no mountain high enough."

Having been married with children for some time now, I know how important it is to keep things fun and interesting. One way I like to do this is to kiss the hubby in front of the kids. This does a couple of things: 1) Lets them see you love each other. 2) Grosses them out; which then inspires me to tell them that I think it would be nice to relive our wedding kiss in front of their friends. After all, we did kiss in front of a group of people when we wed. They are then filled with terror at the prospect of such a sight. This is a good time to ask them to clean their rooms. (Isn't parenting fun?)

The Great Outdoors

When my husband and I built our house, we had long discussions as to whether or not we would someday like to have either a place at a lake, or a pool at home.

As a child, I would go to the lake with my grandparents. I can remember jumping off of the pier and swimming to the raft. My grandmother would take us on walks to the cemetery and we would look for the oldest gravestone. We would look for four-leaf clovers. My grandfather would go fishing and we would have fresh fish for dinner. I look back at those times fondly.

When I was an adult, we went to the lake a couple times to see my father's place there. We took rides in the pontoon boat. However, I had grown up and I found that I no longer wanted to get in the water. I couldn't see the bottom and the thought of swimming with fish now seemed gross.

So we made the decision to put in a pool instead of finding a place at the lake. It is more convenient to simply walk outside. No travel needed. When you have three kids in tow, convenience is key. (It's also nice to have the pool, particularly when I enjoy it by myself. I secretly wish I could open my pool and charge admission to the general public, for the sole purpose of being able to pay some kid to refill my drink for me, so I don't have to get up from reading my book to do it myself.)

When my oldest child was in the fourth grade, one of the projects they were assigned was a report on something in Indiana. She did her project on Clifty Falls, near Madison, Indiana. We thought it would be nice to take her to that park over the summer, so she could see the falls. We also thought it would make a good photography project for 4H, thus killing two birds with one stone.

I should preface this with three points:

1. We do not rough it when vacationing. Our idea of roughing it is when the satellite goes out during a storm. We do NOT camp, ever.

2. This was our first time anywhere near hiking trails.

3. The ages of our children at this time were 10, 8, and 3. At the time, the three-year-old was still in a stroller when we went anywhere.

We arrived at Clifty Falls and checked into our hotel. (Do not judge. Refer to point 1.) We received a map of the trails at check-in, and my husband (who, normally, is brilliant) studied it, and announced that we should do the first trail before dinner.

So he went to the car for the stroller.

I said, "What are you doing?"

He said, "Getting the stroller for the boy. The sign says it's easy."

I said, "Does it also say it's paved?"

So along we go, our son in a stroller, walking through the "easy" trail, which of course, was not paved, not even close. The trail curved, and took us uphill then back to the road. Our daughters were out-hiking us by a landslide, so much so that we had to keep telling them to slow down and wait for us.

State parks are very … green. Do you know what green stuff grows in the woods? Poison ivy. I yelled at the girls to look at nature with their eyes and not with their hands. We did not want to deal with poison ivy. My husband then tried to explain to me the chances of them actually being allergic to poison ivy, even if they came into contact with it. I tried to listen while pushing the boy in a stroller, uphill, over branches and roots.

Then my husband pushed my fear button. He looked around and said, "Does this kind of remind you of the movie 'The Fugitive'? You know, when the train crashes, and they are all escaping in the woods?"

It suddenly became very important that we get out to civilization, and soon. There were no other people on this trail with us; we had no idea what was in these woods. We needed to get on a paved road and get to a restaurant, quickly.

Also, the trail was becoming a bit more taxing, not easy. Apparently, the person who labeled the trail "easy" had no idea how heavy a toddler in a stroller could be on an unimproved trail. Finally, I asked my son to get out of the stroller and walk. He didn't want to. I then informed him that there was a chance we wouldn't make it out of the woods alive if he didn't get out and walk. Needless to say, he got out, and we started hightailing it out of the woods.

The next day, we were to see the falls. We drove to where the lookout was. We walked the bit of trail to get to the falls, which was a ways, and took the required picture. We then got back in the car and drove to the next one, and the next one, and the next one. This went on until all the falls were seen, and we were ready to head to civilization: the amusement park.

What can I say? While I do enjoy all of God's creations, and I think every bit of it is beautiful, I'm a city girl at heart. Plus, I really enjoy the blue ice cream. You can't get that in the woods.

Amusement parks are really more my speed, unlike trails and nature. I like to watch all the people. I like knowing that if we get hungry, we aren't going to have to guess if the food is edible or poisonous. If there's a water park, we can see the bottom of the water, with no fish nipping at your toes. The lines for rides are an exercise in patience, but the blue ice cream helps.

Since I live in a house surrounded by cornfields and trees, with a few houses mixed in, a vacation is getting to see something different and new. I don't lie in the grass and look at the clouds and pick out shapes like I did when I was a kid, but that's only because I now know there are bugs in the grass. So I look at clouds, I just need a lawn chair.

I like the great outdoors; I just prefer to observe it from a distance.

Stay At Home Mom Tribulations: Who's The Boss?

Waking Up Mom

As a mother, you can be awakened by a plethora of things. I have woken up to babies crying, to children getting sick in the bathroom, to the sound of the house settling, and once, to an earthquake. I thought someone had turned the washer on. (I figured it had to be an earthquake, because those happen more frequently than anyone else in the house doing laundry.)

My FAVORITE way to wake up is how I'm awakened each morning when hubby gets up with the kids. It usually goes a little something like this.

Megan softly walks in and throws herself over me and hugs me and kisses me and says, "Mommy, I love you. We are going to school."

My reply is always, "Oh dolly, I love you too. I'll be right down to tell everyone goodbye."

Then she gives me a hand to help me up. The old body creaks and cracks, and I trudge down the stairs to hug and kiss each of my children before they leave for school. I always watch until they are safely on the bus, then I look around and think, "I'm not sure what I did to deserve that, but thank you Lord, for those gifts. What do you have planned for me today?"

Perhaps I'm a little sappy. The world now knows that I'm a terrible cook and I only clean and do laundry grudgingly, but I believe God gave me the idea of the days-of-the-week meals to make cooking dinner fun for all of us, because I do enjoy it more now. And it doesn't bother me too much to do the laundry and clean up things when no one else does.

They may not show it all the time, but they do appreciate me. They appreciate me so much that I have not been to the restroom by myself since 1995.

You should know that I am usually reading two books at once, and the best place to read is the bathroom. Everyone knows this, whether they own up to it or not. Therefore, I keep books both upstairs and downstairs for when I get the urge to you know... read. My restrooms are also stocked with a plethora of magazines and catalogs.

As a child, I was taught to go to the restroom in pairs, for safety reasons. As teenagers, we traveled in packs to the bathroom to talk about boys. I believe this is all preparation for marriage and children. Once you have them, you will never attend alone. They either walk right in, or knock until you have no choice but to answer.

In my house it usually goes something like this:

<knock knock>

Me: Yes?

Kid 1: Can you do my hair?

Me: Um, no, I'm busy at the moment.

Kid 1: OK.

<knock knock>

Me: What?

Kid 3: The girls won't play with me!

Me: Can I do something about that later?

Kid 3: OK.

<knock knock>

Me: WHAT IS IT?

Kid 2: Man, grouch. I was just asking when we are going to eat.

Me: When you learn to cook.

<knock knock>

Me: GOOD GRIEF — WHAT???

Kid 1: Whatcha doin'?

Me: My taxes. Go away!

Sometimes I wish I were invisible. This evening, after discovering that I have ballooned to a weight that doesn't permit me to fit into a single pair of shorts from last summer, I went for a walk with my iPod. When I walk, I like to listen to music that keeps me moving. Sometimes the music moves me and I feel like dancing, or playing the air guitar, or air keyboard, or in general, making a fool of myself. These are the moments when I wish I were invisible. I live in a neighborhood that has a lot of people that like to go out and enjoy the weather. A LOT of people were out on this evening, prohibiting me from having a walk/rock out session, thereby, enforcing the need to be invisible.

Unfortunately for me, I'm only invisible when it's inconvenient. Mothers who have seen the video of the invisible woman/mother can understand what I'm saying. At bedtime I tell the kids, "Turn off the TV, get off the computer, get ready for bed." This falls on deaf ears. I will also tell them to bring the laundry down, or pick up their things. They can't hear me because I'm invisible and I have no sound emitting from me. Sometimes they just do not understand what I'm saying because I have broken out into Dutch, a language they do not understand. I have no idea that I'm doing it. This is very inconvenient.

I guess being invisible can only occur inconveniently. It's like being in school all over again. Being invisible, when all you dream of is standing out in a crowd. I prefer to blend in, or be invisible, for those lone walks around the block, when just the right song comes on the iPod.

Hats

Today I was thinking of all the hats we wear as parents. In any given week, I am chef (I do cook on occasion, not that anyone wants to eat it), taxi driver, tutor, librarian, hairdresser, personal shopper, stylist, secretary, editor, entertainment planner, therapist, and housekeeper. The list could go on, of course.

Like birthday parties. I love to throw a kid party. However, I secretly believe that the mom is the one who should get the party instead of the kid. After all, we are the ones who carried them for nine months, gave birth to them, changed their diapers, fed them, clothed them, and did all the work. They… showed up crying and have complained ever since.

But no matter what hat you are wearing, the important things to remember are these:

God has entrusted you to be your children's parent, guidance counselor, and the one to love them, regardless of anything else.

You are the only people that will ever love your children as much as God. Even though you love them, your love will never compare to His love for them.

Wear your hats with love and respect for this awesome responsibility bestowed upon you.

An Exchange of Wills

Raising children is an exchange of wills. Both parties want something from each other and figure out trades to accomplish each person's desires. In my house, we have come up with a trade recently that makes everyone happy. Here is how the exchange works.

In the morning, I don't like seeing their beds unmade. I also don't like the breakfast dishes left on the floor. My children don't like riding the bus home. They say it's like the "Sixteen Candles" bus. So we have worked out a trade that if they do morning chores, I will pick them up from school. If it's not done ... sorry, it's "Sixteen Candles" for you, and not just one of you, but all three of you. That way, they keep each other accountable. This is an exchange of wills that mostly works out in my favor.

Mom Never Told Me

Things mom never told me, about being a mom:

1. It's your fault. It doesn't matter what the situation, and doesn't even matter if you were there, it is your fault.

2. If something is missing, you hid it from sight to spite them. It is your job to find it.

3. Laundry miraculously gets washed, dried, folded, and put away. You have nothing to do with it; therefore, why should they thank you? Also, if it's not done, it's your fault.

4. You will need to remember everything you have ever learned in school. You are not allowed to have forgotten anything. If you forget how to do something, you are considered stupid.

5. Food just happens. You will need to make sure it is ready, or if it's not ready in time for the stomach growling, you will need to have a backup plan. (I like to refer to my backup plan as "going out tonight.")

6. You will either have to get up before everyone else to get a hot shower, or wait at least an hour after everyone is gone for the water to replenish to a temperature above Arctic Ocean.

Stories by My Middle Child

When my middle child was little, she had a speech delay. This was very frustrating, because we were often playing a guessing game to figure out what she wanted. It was even more frustrating for her. We put her in preschool early, thinking that the social interaction would help her. The preschool was convinced that she had hearing problems. What we found out was that her hearing was very good, and quite selective. She is good at tuning out, which she still does to this day.

During this time, she would throw fits and throw herself to the ground. She would pull her hair from her head in fits of despair. Finally, when she was four, after speech therapy, and fantastic teachers, she began speaking… and hasn't stopped. The only time she shuts down is when she is upset. When she began speaking, however, we also found that she had a big imagination. She had thirteen imaginary friends, each of them with their own names; one of them was a pet.

Eventually, she grew out of this, but she was also a performer. She would dance and sing. She would tell stories. The stories have stuck around. She's a creative type who needs an outlet for her creativity, and also I think she just gets bored. The following are some of her stories.

In fourth grade, she decided she liked boys. One boy in particular struck her fancy. He was a year older than her in school, and they went to different schools. I found this "relationship" to be harmless because they never saw each other, except in passing on the bus. One day, she came home and said that she was going to have to break up with him because he touched her hair on the bus, and she just wouldn't tolerate that kind of behavior. I told her that I was sure that he was reasonable, and if she told him that she didn't like her hair messed with, he would leave it alone.

This went on for a few weeks. She seemed happy because she had a boyfriend, and I was happy that it was one she saw for five minutes a day at best. Then one day it came out that the entire thing was a story she'd made up.

When she was in sixth grade, we were sitting in a pizzeria waiting for our food when she dropped the bomb that she was sent to the principal's office that day for talking. We asked her a number of questions about it. She actually started crying. While her father questioned her, I observed. When he offered to go in and ask about it, she said no. I then looked her square in the eye and asked her if she was making up the entire thing. I stared her down. Then she cracked, and said she was. She wiped her tears, looked around at our astonished faces, and said, "See, I told you I was a good actress."

This year, she was upset because she didn't get the part she wanted in the school play. She was upset, even though she assured me that she was happy to be an extra, because it was better than being cut altogether. She was also having cramps due to her monthly, making her even more squirrely than usual. Which leads us to the next story.

While in her drama class one day, she had a fit, so her teacher decided to talk to her to find out what was going on. She then explained to the teacher that she had been stabbed at a Red Lobster when she was little and that she was scared because the man who had done it was going to get out of jail soon. This fiction, of course, led to a phone call from the teacher, who was concerned for my daughter's well-being. I had to go in and talk to the teacher and take the child with me so she could set things straight.

I assured the poor teacher that it was all made up. Being her mother, and having been with her every day of her life except for church camp, I was sure that if my daughter had been stabbed, I would have remembered it. What did happen was that my daughter was embarrassed by the truth and too scared to share her feelings. We discussed it all. My daughter apologized for lying. The teacher then informed her that the story would be a good one to write for English class.

We have discussed lying. I don't think she comes up with these things out of spite. I think she has an overactive imagination, gets bored, and needs a release. I thought drama club would provide that release. Apparently, when you're an extra, you do not have enough to do to get that release.

I have no idea what her next story will be. I can only hope that when she comes up with it, she will use it to get an A on her next English assignment. Either way, it never gets boring with her around.

Discipline and Growing Adults

When I was a little girl and I went out to play with friends, I had to be home before dark. I would test this some nights and get home at dusk, until my mother told me about a little girl that was abducted going home from her neighbor's house after dark. I wasn't sure if that was true, but I wasn't willing to test it. So usually, I made it before dusk. And once I discovered Ricky Schroder on "Silver Spoons," it was a non-issue, because I had to be home in time to see my show.

I had my first job when I was probably 11 years old, selling discount cards for a tire store. My next job came at 15, when I started working at the mall. I also cleaned our house for as long as I can remember. I was always taught that you work, then you get paid. If you don't work, you don't get paid. Easy enough.

But I wasn't taught what to do with the money once I had it. Of course, I spent it till it was gone. When I was sixteen, I was given a car, with the stipulation that I would have to work to pay for the insurance and gas.

I wasn't allowed to date until I was sixteen. Even requests for group dates got a resounding "no" until then. My bedtime on school nights was 9:00 p.m., until I graduated from high school. When I started dating, I was allowed to be out on the weekend until 11:00 p.m., until college, when I was dating the man I eventually married. Then my curfew moved to midnight, and then it was extended to 1:00 a.m. But I am not sure that counted, because usually I fell asleep in the car on the way home anyway.

My mother was fairly strict, by some people's standards. She didn't tolerate disrespect and I'm pretty sure time-outs were not invented yet, because I just got my hind-end beat. She got her message across this way, and eventually I learned how far I could go without pushing her to the edge. Not that I always stopped in time, but I knew that there were consequences to my behavior.

I didn't have my first drink of alcohol until I was 21. My entire family on my mother's side, and half of the relatives on my father's side, were smokers, and I never once picked up a cigarette. I never got into any trouble in school, and while my mouth would get me into trouble at home at times, I was a good kid.

All of those same rules apply in my household—with the exception that I would prefer if they didn't date until they were out of college. This is not a popular opinion in our house, but we haven't crossed that bridge yet. We do not buy our children things whenever they want them. They either work to pay for them or save birthday money for the things they want. If they don't do chores, they don't get paid. The reality of life is if you don't work, you don't get paid. It's a simple life lesson every kid needs to learn.

My children hear the word "no" regularly and learn that they can't always get their way. We do not drink in front of our children; we might have a handful of drinks in a year, anyway. Neither my husband nor I smoke. The kids know that there are alcoholics in my family and that grandma died from cancer caused from smoking.

When they get too big for their britches, I remind them that they are the children, not the adults. I also know that (as Dave Ramsey once said) I am raising them to be adults, not children. If we raise our children to continue to be children, we are going to raise an entire generation of 40-year-old "kids" who live in their parent's basements and sponge off them till their parents die. (I don't have a basement just for this reason.) While they are sure to receive an inheritance when we die, WE aren't working hard now so they don't have to work, especially when they are old enough to take care of themselves.

I believe that too many parents today try so hard to be friends with their kids that they forget that their main job is to parent them. When my children were younger and were mad at me they would say, "You're not my friend anymore!" To which I would say, "God did not put me on this earth to be your friend. He put me here to be your mother. He has given you friends and me friends. When you are grown to the person God wants you to be, THEN we will be friends. Until then, I am your mother and my job is to educate you and care for you. You are getting a free education. So say thank you."

I am not sure when it became the custom in society to not discipline kids, or when parents got so worried about hurting their children's feelings that they lost the ability to say no. Perhaps if more parents used the word, we would have fewer boys walking around with their pants sagging so low that a strong breeze would make them fall around their ankles.

The Bible says, in Proverbs 22:6, "Train a child in the way he should go, and when he is old he will not turn from it." In Proverbs 29:15, "The rod and the rebuke give wisdom, but a child left to himself brings shame to his mother."

The instructions are in the Bible. I don't want to raise 40-year-old children who never leave home and can't provide for themselves. As much as I love my children and feel sorrow in thinking about their one day growing up and leaving the nest, I want them to experience their own lives more. I want them to respect authority. I want them to work hard for the things they want and need.

I also want them to be everything God created them to be. They need to know that disappointments come with the territory. There are no silver platters that are going to be handed to them with all of their dreams come true. They are going to have to work for them.

Field Trips

I'm a city girl without a city. I was born in a small town, probably die in a small town (you know the song, right?). That's probably where they'll bury me. I went on a field trip to the 4H Fairgrounds with my son recently. My friend Jessica convinced me to come. Yes, it was as exciting as it sounds.

First, I get on a bus with three classrooms full of kids (taking note to NEVER become a bus driver). This is how the ride goes. I didn't remember having so little leg room on a school bus. I'm in charge of five kids, so throughout the ride all I say is, "Girls, sit down... boys, sit up. Jessica, having fun? Girls, sit down... Boys, sit up." This is because the girls keep getting on their knees to see around the boys, who keep slouching so they're almost falling out of the seat.

I'm also curious as to why the driver is the only one who gets a seatbelt. I would think that it's for the following reasons: 1. To restrain the one adult (who is normally in a large vehicle alone with all the kids) from losing it, or 2. If there were a terrible accident, they would be the only one to survive, which would be their reward for the restraint they show in their job. One would think the kids would have seatbelts, if only to keep them in the seat. But what do I know?

Finally, we arrive at the fairgrounds, and we are divided up into groups, each with 10 children. Jessica and I are relieved that we get to walk together. Our plan is that she keeps an eye out while I do the yelling. I tell the kids before we leave the bus area that if they stray and don't listen, I have no problem with letting the cows take a bite out of them. (Of course, I was kidding, but they didn't know that.)

The kids are amazed at the animals and want to touch every one of them. I'm kicking myself for not bringing hand sanitizer, and look around for something that will prevent diseases.

Then we get to see a sheep sheared, so we sit in the stands, where the children immediately go to the top row. (Have I mentioned that I'm old, and a klutz, and even at movies when there are stairs, I don't go to the top?) With help, I get to the top, but by the time I get there, the kids, of course, climb down. Then they go down front, getting all mixed up with other kids from different groups, to get a closer look.

The sheep are led in on a rope leash from a pen, from which they want to escape. They are then tied to a pole and held still, by fellows that may be actual ranch hands. Then the sheep get shorn like... well, sheep. When they realize they are naked, I imagine they are relieved to be cool, yet a bit embarrassed by their current state. Then they try to get away, but are led by their rope to another pen to watch their friends suffer the same fate.

With the top row open for new adventurers, a couple of girls who are not in my group decide to stand on the very top row. When I tell them to sit down, they look at me like I'm nuts and ignore me. I then vow that if they fall, I will simply point and laugh, and tell them that they should have listened.

We eventually make our way out of the building, which at this point may actually be awakening my lost sense of smell. (After having children, my sense of smell seems to have disappeared, which makes me a good candidate to work in the nursery at church, because I don't smell the diapers.)

Having all of these animals in what seems like a large barn from the outside, but is actually much smaller inside, especially when they are all dropping manure wherever, is a new experience. I'm not sure why I get to smell this, but not cake, other than the fact that I don't bake, but it doesn't smell good.

We get a few pictures by the combine and the tractor and we get back on the bus. The bus now seems like a great comfort as it takes us back to school, or at least closer to civilization, and potentially, cake. Plus, Jessica and I have decided we deserve a frappuccino for our hard work.

The Old Mom

It occurred to me that when my youngest child entered kindergarten, that I was now the "old" mom. I admit that the spacing of my children is part of what gives me this title. My oldest is in high school, my middle in junior high, and my baby is in second grade. As I looked around at all these young mothers waiting to go on a field trip, with what could only be their oldest child, based on my assessment of their ages, I was struck by the finality of it. These mothers were just getting started on this journey. I am still in the middle of mine; my days of waking up with babies and dealing with diapers (and toting a small arsenal of supplies around just for a trip to the store) are over.

I remember being a young mother. When we left the hospital with our first child, I sat in the back seat of the car with the baby. As my husband pulled away from the curb, I said, "Wow, they really will give just anyone a baby, won't they?"

I was FAR from prepared. Sure, I'd read the books, I had taken the prenatal classes, but I lovingly refer to my oldest child as the guinea pig. I hadn't a clue as to what I was doing, so I made the most mistakes with her. Fortunately, she has become a lovely young lady, no thanks to me. I believe the amount of therapy she will need (after enduring my show-tune singing and parking her in front of Barney) will be minimal at best.

We got pregnant very quickly with her, and I gained 60 pounds. I figured since I was going to be pregnant, I may as well look the part. Ben and Jerry were my support. But by the end, I looked like I had swallowed at least two basketballs. I was mostly a failure as a pregnant woman. When I went for ultrasounds, I was convinced I was going to give birth to a peanut-shaped turtle. I never could see the baby in the picture. When I had each of the kids, I didn't have my glasses on, so I had to wait an hour afterwards to see that they were in fact human.

Nine months later, we were blessed with a beautiful, healthy little girl, exactly on her due date and not a moment before. To this day, she does things in her own time, whether you are running late or not. She brings me more joy than I thought imaginable. Proving that what I was seeking in this life wasn't status, but family.

Now that she is in high school, and my middle child is in junior high, there are some topics that you are not allowed to discuss in front of them. Any amount of PDA completely grosses them out. My husband and I make it a point to hug and kiss each other and tell each other we love one another in front of them. Any little peck will result in cries of, "OH GROSS! Get a room, would you?"

To which our reply is always, "Uh, hello? We have one, we are in it. In fact, every room in the house is ours. Which one do you want us to go to?"

Grossing them out is a perk, of course, but we do this because we feel it's important for them to see that mom and dad are in a good place and that we love each other. We may tease each other or frustrate each other (like when he puts his dirty laundry just outside the hamper, or I get into a self-esteem funk), but love is the basis of all of it and that's what brings us together as a family.

My son is eight. My girls got the scared, "Please don't cry, why don't you listen, what can I do, I'm messing this up" mommy. My son got the relaxed "I'm old, you'll live if you fall down; sure, spill something on the floor, it needs to be cleaned anyway; if you want to eat Cheerios from the floor, the ten second rule applies here, go ahead; stick the binky in diet soda to clean it off and give it back" mommy.

He is, in turn, a pretty relaxed kid. Thankfully so. He sat through dance lessons, dance recitals, softball games, band and orchestra concerts, and who knows what else. He doesn't complain. You just hand him an electronic screen, and he plays his games. He also plays basketball, soccer, baseball, and likes to draw.

He is also the peacemaker of the family. He tells me when the girls are fighting (usually they are; we are still waiting for the friendship to take hold). Unless someone is in pain because they get into a knock-down drag-out fight, I don't interfere. I figure if no one is bleeding or on fire, they need to learn to work it out themselves. Unless, of course, they mess with my baby (who is now eight, not two like he is in my mind, and who may have instigated it anyway, because he is his father's son), then I come unglued. He is also very smart and kind, and of course handsome, but he's my baby. My last go-round.

When my youngest turns ten, I may need a Valium sandwich to get through it. Plus, I'll be forty that same year. My oldest will be driving by then, so I may already be on medication.

They are growing up entirely too fast. I'm pretty sure that I'm not finished growing up yet. How can they be catching up so fast? Yesterday I was in high school; today I have a child in high school. When I was fifteen, I was sure I was an adult.
I tell my fifteen-year-old that she is still a kid, and to embrace it. The way I figure it, you have your entire life to be an adult. There is no going back. You get this one chance to be a kid and you should hold on to it as long as you can, at least till college. Then you can start figuring some things out.

****

Questions from a six year old

Six year old: Mom, do dinosaurs have boobs?

Me: I don't know, but I think that the mommy dinosaur would, to feed the baby. And let's not say boobs anymore, please.

Six year old: Well mom, on "Punky Brewster," Punky goes up to Henry and says, "Henry, I'm getting boobs," and now Megan says that 'cause she thinks it's funny.

Me: I understand. However, Megan is a girl and she will be told not to say that in front of you anymore.

Six year old: Is Shamu a boy or a girl?

Me: I don't know, but I think Shamu must be a girl, because did you see all the water that whale was retaining? That thing looked like I feel a week out of every month.

Six year old: But mom, I thought Shamu was a boy?

Me: Well, that explains why it gets such great service, and why no one ever mentions that he needs to lose weight.

****

Singing

I love to sing. If you have witnessed this, you also know that I do not sing well. However, I like to sing in church. I try to position myself where I'm surrounded by people who also like to sing in church, and then I sing just loud enough to participate without making a fool of myself.

This, my friend, is a catch-22. Because... A) If you sit beside people who sing like they just stepped on a stage (as many of these people do), you want to just be quiet and listen to them. Thereby making them wonder why you don't sing and if you just aren't feeling the beat. B) If you do sing beside these people and they do hear you, they will do one of two things: 1) Sing loud enough to drown you out (which I appreciate), or 2) They stop singing altogether and look around trying to find where the howling is coming from. Church is why lip synching was invented in the first place.

I am the best Jackson Five singer ever, at least, in my own mind. My daughter got a Jackson 5 CD for her birthday, so we listen to it a lot in the car. (As you know, the car is my site of choice for singing.) Of course, back in those days you could make out all the words in songs. Therefore, I can sing "ABC" with the best of them.

I will admit I'm not as good at singing along to newer music. It's a little more difficult to get ALL the words right, but I do give it my best shot. Sometimes I just have to make up the part I don't know. Kind of like in the song "Jack and Diane," where I used to sing "make us go swimmin' and then," and the actual words are "make us women and men." It does make much more sense with the actual words. But the kids don't mind when you sing as badly as I do; the real lyrics don't matter, it's all perfect torture. I see myself as fabulous, so I will always keep attempting to make a joyful noise, even if I'm the only one made joyful by the noise I create.

In my beautiful, practically empty rooms, the acoustics are great. I've discovered that sock skating on the floors and singing in such a room actually makes me sound better. Of course, I always sound better when no one is around to hear me. It's similar to the whole "if a tree falls in a forest" thing. Does the tree make a sound? Do I sound better? The world may never know.

Isn't That Just the Way It Goes?

Today we have laundry on the coffee table, the kitchen island is covered with junk, the kids are already in their pajamas at 7 p.m., and my hubby is relaxing in the pool. So of course, today is the day that the neighbor's college kid shows up wanting to talk to us, because she was selling encyclopedias. So I said sure, come on in and sit down, look at our folded underwear. After all, I am nothing if not hospitable.

I would like to add that in addition to not buying these books that are "better than encyclopedias," (which cost a whopping $490—Hello? Ever heard of Google?), my cat took a liking to her and proceeded to shed excessively all over her and her bag.

I should probably start folding laundry in another room other than my "receiving room" and offer lemonade to guests, and have my child play the piano for entertainment. Yeah, I don't even sell myself on that one. I don't have lemonade unless it's from a two-liter bottle or a can, and truly, no one stops by here to begin with, making my laundry folding a non-issue. Also, doesn't everyone have their kids in pajamas by 7 p.m. on the first night of summer break? I see no reason to stop all signs of decorum right away, after all. It could shock their systems to change habits so quickly.

If you do plan on showing up at my house unannounced, be forewarned that I too tend to get into my PJs quite early, and tend to stay that way well into the late morning, if at all possible.

Notes

1. It doesn't matter how late you stay up if you drink a gallon of diet soda in a day. You will have to get up before 9 a.m. to use the restroom, thus ruining the dream of sleeping in until 10 a.m. This is when you would wake if you could, fully refreshed and ready to face the day. P.S. I would like to clarify that Big Sexy hairspray does not keep hair big and sexy once you sleep on it. When waking, Big Sexy hair looks like a fluffy cat that has just fallen in water.

2. You know you are a good mom when: Your kids get themselves up and have donut sticks and brownies for breakfast. But it's OK, because they will throw the wrappers away, and besides, it was all the six-year-old's idea. And we all know that whatever the six-year-old says, goes.

3. In our house we have had (at different points) 3 cats, 1 hamster, 4 birds, a newt, and countless fish. As the Cat in the Hat would say, we take them home, love them for two weeks and then... NOTHING! I think that perhaps the virtual pet idea is a good one. Think of the money you could save. Fifteen dollars for an electronic pet. You don't have to buy it food or even look at it if you don't want to. My advice is, don't get any pets until you've tried the electronic ones. Let

the kids try and keep those alive first.

4. When I was a child, I had to get myself ready for school and wait for the bus. I never knew if there was a delay or cancellation. The rest of the kids in my neighborhood had parents at home or would somehow get the memo on these events. I would stand out there waiting to go to school while they made fun of me. I think maybe this problem could have been averted if I had had the Internet. The computer I had as a child was only useful if you wanted to play Pong. Today you can get online and see, in a matter of seconds, if there is a delay or cancellation. You can listen to the radio or see it on TV. The radio and TV option may have been there when I was a child, but I was too busy trying to get ready and out the door to realize it. This is why the Internet is so important.

Teenagers: The Reason God Gave Us Pharmacies

Teenagers, Driving, and Jell-O

Not so long ago, I received a text message from a friend. She had seen a sign that made her think of me. The sign said "Raising teenagers is like trying to nail Jell-O to a wall." I said that it sounded about right.

My oldest now has her learner's permit. I love her. I'm afraid she may kill us, but I love her. Here's the thing: I am not a patient person. I do not have a knack for teaching someone to drive a moving vehicle. (Truth be told, I don't even really enjoy driving myself. I drive out of necessity.) Also, it stresses her out to try to learn from us. We're yelling things like "Don't put us in the grass!" and "Not too far over! Do you want us to get hit by oncoming traffic?" It is impossible for any of us to relax.

I think driver's ed instructors should be given some sort of medal of valor or something. They could be knighted, if we still did that.

I do want her to learn to drive. I have thought this over, and I realize all the perks to having another driver in the house. She can run to town and grab things at the store for us. She can pick up a pizza. She can take her siblings to and from school. The possibilities are endless.

On the other hand, like I said, the possibilities are endless. She could have a wreck. I had a wreck not long after I got my license. What if she got hurt? I couldn't stand it. Plus, it requires me to let go. I'm not really a fan of letting go. I'm more of a choke-hold kind of person. I latch on and hold on for dear life.

That also means that I am a teenager's worst nightmare. I ask questions. I look at them and see the little girls they once were, not the young ladies that they are. The time goes so quickly. Yesterday, they were riding around in Barbie Jeeps, and today one is learning to drive an actual car. One day they are learning to make chocolate milk, and the next day they are learning chemical equations.

I still ask what they have for lunch and who they sat by at lunch. I'm supposed to ask which boy they think has the cutest smile. I'm supposed to be getting in shape and getting crazy strong so I can scare prospective dates away. So far, they only like boys who are in the movies. I prefer this. Boys at school have little to offer in their eyes. I am quite certain they are correct in their assumptions of them, as I was once a teenage girl, and I know about teenage boys.

When my oldest turned ten, I cried. Double digits are the beginning of the end. It seems like yesterday and a lifetime ago, all at the same time. Teenagers. Trying to take care of them, teach them, and let them go. As easy as nailing Jell-O to a wall. It's hard on the parents, and on them. It's hard being in that space between child and adult. It's even harder seeing them as growing up, and no longer children.

I think they will always be, in my mind, children. I just have to get to the place where they can become adults, not just grown children. As adults, we drive.

I think I will start pricing fruit baskets. The driver's ed instructor is going to deserve one.

Teenagers and Secret Survivor Societies

I was discussing in church recently that I may need a mentor mom. So far, I have no volunteers. I believe I've figured out why. I have two teenage daughters who are just nineteen months apart.

(Yes, that was on purpose. Don't laugh; I'm an only child. I didn't know better. You see, my theory went a little something like this: We should have two, and have them close together. Then they would be close, built-in best friends for life. They would never long for someone to play with. They would never be lonely. I was lonely for a lot of my childhood, watching shows like "The Brady Bunch" and "Growing Pains" and wondering how much better my life would be with siblings to go through the trauma of growing up. Like I said, I didn't know any better.)

This is what I have discovered. It's not hard to get a mentor mom if you are the mom of a baby or a toddler. Those blissful years are nothing compared to the teenage years. Diapers and the lack of a vocabulary are your friends at this point; embrace them! As soon as they hit about 9, it all starts going downhill from there, and the vocabulary just increases in ways you don't want to think about.

I think perhaps that women who have lived through their children's teenage years (with girls especially) have formed a secret society of sorts. They are all sitting around in their little clubs, watching the rest of us flail around, and enjoying the show. They won't get involved because they have already lived through their fair share of drama. (It's either that or they are mostly institutionalized.)

A friend of mine suggests that perhaps they are sitting around sipping their drinks and waiting for the next survivor to arrive. I am not a drinker, so I said, "What will I do? Learn to drink?"

She said, "Well, I didn't say they are drinking alcoholic drinks. You could have an orange mint julep." I asked her what that was. Apparently that is what Reese Witherspoon served at her wedding. It's some kind of a southern drink. I persisted in asking what exactly this was. Her reply was, "I don't know, I don't live there!"

My friend has two daughters. Neither of which are yet into the teenage stage. While I love her dearly, if she had teenagers herself, she'd understand that perhaps I may need to learn to drink. And as to whatever an orange mint julep is, it may not be enough to get me through this stage of life. But I am willing to give it a try at this point.

There was a time when my daughters wanted to share a room. I refused to let them and told them that they would thank me later. At this point, they practically need written permission to enter the other one's room. Can you imagine what it would be like if they did, in fact, have to share a room? I see duct tape running down the center of the room and intense fighting if so much as a shoelace crossed over into the other's domain. There could be anarchy. There would, of course, have to be squares of duct tape on the floor also, to denote neutral territory.

Don't get me wrong; there are times when they get along. Those times are far and few between. They can be sitting on the same sofa watching a show together, getting along just fine, then one moves or looks at the other wrong. And then it's "ON LIKE DONKEY KONG." Hide the breakables. Call in the National Guard. SOMEONE BLEW BUBBLE GUM BUBBLES IN THE OTHER'S PRESENCE! This cannot be tolerated. We must go to war!

I have tried entering into peace talks with them. I don't know what to do. I have told them that I cannot possibly live forever. They are going to have to learn to get along. If their father and I survive the teenage years, we fully intend to move to Florida without leaving a forwarding address until they figure out how to get along.

I can only imagine what our family gatherings will look like if they don't figure this out. Will we have to have separate family gatherings because even their husbands and children won't like each other? Am I required to buy the Bob Evans dinner twice for Thanksgiving? Clean the house twice? Put a line of duct tape down the middle of the house in order to have them all over at the same time, but quarantine them to separate parts of the house, with only the bathrooms being neutral? It's too much!

This is why I need a mentor mom. My own mother is now gone, but I don't think she could have helped me with this one. She only had me. She didn't have to deal with any squabbling kids. She could have perhaps thought back to when she was growing up with all of her brothers and sisters.

But I tend to think maybe that's why she had just the one. She remembered all too well.

I do have a mother-in-law that raised daughters. She is busy, though. Maybe she doesn't want me to know if and when it does get better. I think for the most part, my sisters-in-law get along. But maybe the secret is in how long that took to happen. She may think that if she doesn't tell me this, then if it happens sooner for my girls, I'll be pleasantly surprised. If it happens later, then she didn't give me false hope.

In the meantime, I guess I'm in this alone. If you want to apply to be my mentor mom, feel free to do so. I would greatly appreciate it. If not, I think I understand. Just get my chair ready at the table and have my orange mint julep poured. I'll be anxious to figure out what that tastes like. Until that day, I will make do with ice cream. (I sure hope the secret society comes with a free gym membership.)

Teenage Girls, John Hughes, Dating, and Me

If it's not one thing, it's another. Someone was in someone else's room; someone borrowed a shirt without asking; someone looked at someone wrong. And that's just between the teenage girls. Mix in two parents and stir in a little brother and you have all the makings of a reality show.

My husband, while he is a wonderful husband and equally wonderful father, likes to tease the children. He is actually the instigator. When the girls were young, the three of them were the best of friends, but they are older now and somehow have lost the camaraderie that they once shared. Dad isn't as funny as he used to be, and the girls aren't as laid back and forgiving as they once were. All of a sudden (or perhaps it only seems all of a sudden to us) they have gone from cute little babies, to adorable funny toddlers, to angsty teenagers overnight.

I have no idea how their personalities can switch at every moment. One minute you are having a perfectly normal conversation with said teen, and the next minute they are madder than a wet hornet. Then you are left wondering what it was you said. Is this normal? Are there research studies being done?

(I am pretty sure I was exactly the same way, although, to get me to own it would take a tremendous amount of coaching. I prefer to look back at my childhood and remember myself as the most perfect child a parent could ever have. I haven't any comparison, so I can claim it; being an only child does have that one perk.)

When my teenage counterparts were all off experimenting with drugs, alcohol, smoking, and/or sex, I was watching television shows where families stayed together, and hoping one day I could be a part of one. While I did have my eye on boys, and thought about them often, I was not particularly interested in any one of them. Boys were for buying you food, so you could avoid salmon-patty night at home, and giving you a ride home so you didn't have to call mom. They really had no other function in my mind.

I was also very busy. I had to plan my wardrobe, and make sure I had the right shoes to go with every outfit. I desperately wanted out of my house. I was sure that if I could only get discovered as the fashion icon I imagined myself to be, I would soon enough end up in Chicago, living my big city life, traveling to buy clothes FOR Bloomingdale's, not just FROM Bloomingdale's. Because of course, when you are the one doing the buying for the big store, I was pretty sure one of the perks would be free clothes.

My own daughters, while they notice certain boys and are fond of them, see them much the same way as I did. They are teenagers, but not yet of dating age. They aren't allowed to even think of being somewhere other than school with a boy. No group dates, no solo dates, period, end of thought. If you can't drive yourself home from any situation you may face, you have no business being there. Any boy who would come to call on one of my daughters will be questioned extensively before she will ever enter a car with him.

I'm thinking of making up a written exam. Such questions that would be required on the exam would be as follows:

1. When driving, where do your hands go? The correct answer would be steering wheel positions ten and two, because your hands do not belong anywhere on my daughter. No holding of the hands, no hand on the thigh. If you are that distracted, you could end up in an accident, and I will hold you personally responsible for any harm that may come to my child because of your stupidity.

2. Do you own your car? Or did your parents pay for it? Did you save money to buy your own car? This shows that you can stick to a goal. If you have everything handed to you on a silver platter, chances are you are going to expect my daughter to hand things to you that you are not going to get. (Side note: My daughters do have very good right-cross punches and will not take kindly to your unwanted advances. Also, if you try something and I find out about it, I will call your mommy.)

Maybe I am getting a little carried away. After all, I did date when I was a teenager. Maybe not as long as some, but I did date, and I had friends who dated a LOT. I know the stories.

My oldest daughter is very close to turning fifteen. My time is running out here. That dating age is approaching swiftly. I can only hope that she will still have her heart set on Daniel Radcliffe.

Right now, she finds all the boys at school very immature and lacking in some form or another. I relish in this. In fact, when I hear stories from my friends about how their daughters have boyfriends or like this boy or another, I chuckle inside. I think, "Better them than me!" How lucky am I that I don't have to deal with all of this. Well, at least, not yet. But without warning, just like the teenage years themselves, it will be upon me.

Some boy whom I haven't met yet or who doesn't even know her yet will one day look up and really see her. He will hear her laugh and think it sounds like church bells on Sunday morning. He will see her smile and think it is as beautiful as the sunrise. He will look into her heart and mind and find what I know is already there: the love and beauty of a thousand angels. Then he will ask her out. All I can say for him is … I hope he tests well.

From Barbie Dolls to Telephone Calls

Yesterday was a big day for us. My second child officially turned into a teenager, making me the mother of not one, but two teenage girls. Those of you with teenage girls will understand the gravity of what I'm saying here. TWO teenage girls. One was hard enough. It's so much drama, all the time. Now there will be two of them.

Not that the younger one hasn't acted like a teenager for at least the last two years, but somehow it's more real now. The idea that the days of Barbie dolls and training bras are going to be morphing into days-long discussions with her friends about boys, terrifies me. No more pigtails, no more Barney (OK, him I could do without), no more cuddles. Now it's all hair straighteners, makeup, and avoiding boys who dress like thugs. What is a mom to do?

I'm completely unprepared for the inevitable. Boys liking my girls. Boys wanting to date my girls. I was once a girl who dated boys, I know what they try. It's disgusting to think about it going on with your own child. They will want to hold hands and worse — kiss them goodnight. UGH! It's too much!

Honestly, I have no idea how this is going to play out. I'm not sure Starbucks is going to get me through this one. Just this last week alone, I had at least four delightfully delicious coffee drinks. I use them as rewards. When I don't have meltdowns, I get a coffee. I figure as long as most of them are nonfat something or other, it can't be that bad, right? Surely it's better than medication. What I probably need is intense therapy so I can come to the understanding that my sweet, precious little babies, who I carried in the womb and have cared for all these years, are growing into young women … who will be doing the same thing in just a few years.

Thirteen years old. It's amazing, really. She is amazing. She weaned herself at ten months old because she wanted to drink from a cup like her sister. She got her first tooth at four months, five months before her sister got hers. The only thing she didn't do first was talk. That came much later. In fact, she was four before she started truly communicating with us. Today she is a musician; she acts in plays, and sings, constantly wowing us with her abilities. She's growing up. She's a character, and I love her more each day.

It seems like yesterday they were both little girls. They are nineteen months apart and they used to get mistaken for twins while riding in their stroller. I used to dress them alike, one in purple, the other in pink. I went from wondering if Huggies were better than Pampers, or if they were both a waste of money and I should just buy Luvs, to getting the right t-shirt with the right name on it, and the right wash of jeans.

The only up side to this entire thing is that they still love Disney and Nickelodeon. In my mind, that keeps them kids. I have always told them they have their whole lives to be adults, but only one chance to be kids, so they'd better be the best kids they can be and have all the fun they can, while they can. When they get old, people will think they are silly for

jumping rope and dancing outside in the yard. They will have to have a fence if they want to see if they can still do a cartwheel. Not that I've ever done that.

I used to love playing with Barbies and riding bikes. I danced in my yard and would sing my heart out. I twirled my baton and lost a tooth eating giant SweetTarts. I want my kids to still do those things and enjoy doing them.

All too soon, it's over and you have to be responsible. I can't play with Barbies now unless I visit a friend with little girls, and I don't ride my bike unless it's for fitness. My dreams have changed, too. I now dream of getting the laundry caught up and getting everyone to find the trash can. But then I wonder if that's really fair. After all, my time has passed. It's their turn now.

Mostly, I think about how I hope they never think like I did, that they can't do something. That they aren't good enough to do it, or that fun careers like writing books or directing movies or acting only happen to people who live in big places, so they shouldn't even try. After all, David Letterman went to Ball State University in Muncie, Indiana. If he can make it from here, so can they. I also hope they never give up on dreaming big, because from big dreams can come big realities. And all my children are wonderfully smart and creative. Just ask me; after all, I'm their mother. I have very little bias.

Foreign Languages?

When I was in high school, I took two years of French. It was either that or Spanish, and I thought French was a more romantic language. Also, my friends were all taking French, so I figured if I needed help with homework, they could help me.

Now, more than two decades later, I only remember how to ask if someone speaks French and how to introduce myself. If I ever go to France, I'll have to dehydrate myself, because I will have no way of asking where the restroom is.

My oldest child is taking Spanish. The first grading period, she did better in Spanish than she did in English. I found this amusing, as English is our native language. I joked about this for some time. Now the two grades are right in line with each other. I might mention that we encouraged her to take the class just so she could order for us at the Mexican restaurant.

We thought it would be a good idea for someone to actually learn a second language. We are fascinated with languages around here. Sometimes, we try to speak with a British accent, sometimes Irish, sometimes Jamaican. Our son once asked us if the people working at the Mexican restaurant were really Mexican or if they were just pretending to be, like we pretend to be British at home.

I also speak Dutch, although I don't realize I'm doing it. It's only when I'm talking to my children. I first noticed this when they were younger and I would discipline them. I would talk to them and they would look at me like I had just dropped from the moon. As they got older, I noticed it happening when I would ask them to do something. Again with the blank stare. Then it occurred to me... they must not be able to understand what I'm saying. I was pretty sure I was speaking English, which as I stated before, IS our native language.

They are old enough to know most, if not all, of the words I was using.So apparently I wasn't speaking English. It's the only explanation.

I was talking about this to a friend of mine, and she said that she had encountered the same type of thing with her children. She mentioned that she asked them if they understood what she was saying, if what was coming out of her mouth was

English, or if in fact she had broken out into Dutch. Apparently they did understand that she was speaking English. I think this can be translated into selective interpretation. They understand what is being said, they just don't translate it into something that applies to them.

Getting Ready

Perhaps I should start this in a positive way, so you will not think that I am a complete failure. My children get up for school every day with alarm clocks. The alarm clocks are set strategically, with at least fifteen minutes between each one so that there aren't fights for the bathroom. They are able to get up and get themselves ready for school, get downstairs for breakfast (which they know how to make) and out the door, in time for the bus. I simply go downstairs to talk to them and see them off. This makes my life significantly easier, as I get a little more sleep during the week. So that we are clear, Monday through Friday, they are able to get ready to leave the house in a timely manner.

I am a college-educated individual. However, I don't spend every waking moment worrying about things I have no control over. I do not get the newspaper. The only time I watch the news is to get the weather forecast. I know that there are bad things that are happening everywhere. I also know that I am not a scientist, a police officer, a government official, or anyone else with the power to solve these problems. All of these things occupy some of my thoughts and time, but they are not the things that plague me.

The thing that keeps me up nights is this: I cannot get the kids up and ready to leave the house on the weekend.

On Saturdays, my son plays basketball. The night before, we discuss what we have to do the next day. I will remind them that they need to set their alarms, set out clothes, or gather up the stuff they need to make sure they are ready to leave the house at a specific time.

On Sundays, we have church. They all know that we have to be there at a certain time, and on one Sunday a month, we have to be there a little earlier, because I have nursery duty. Yet every single Saturday and Sunday, at five or ten minutes after the time I said we were going to leave, I am yelling at them that it is time to go. I realize there are worse things to worry about. I'm certain I can solve this problem. I just can't figure out how.

We have all heard the jokes about how long it takes women to get ready. Obviously, these are jokes by men who don't have children, or perhaps don't realize that women have to not only get themselves ready, but everyone else as well. When my children were younger, I would get them all ready, and then get myself ready. Giving the illusion that it took me longer to get ready. My children are now fourteen, thirteen, and eight. All ages at which they can get themselves ready, unassisted, as they prove every weekday.

I timed myself yesterday to see how long it took me to get ready, if I have no interruptions. From start to finish, with shower, getting dressed, makeup, and hair, it took me twenty five minutes. If I have to share the sink with my husband, give me an additional ten. I think this is pretty good time.

(The main reason I have short hair is because I'm too lazy to be bothered to spend more than five minutes fixing it. I grew up in the 80's. We spent a LOT of time with curling irons to get the right amount of height and curl in our hair. I'm too old for that nonsense. I also believe that my spiky hair distracts from the fact that my nose is crooked and I have crow's feet around my eyes.)

Today, it took my children well over an hour to get ready. That is, without a shower. What they do on weekends is as follows.

1. They wake up and stare at the TV.

2. When I realize they are up and not moving, I get started telling them to get ready.

3. Then they think about it. Maybe they will shower. If they do, then you may as well figure in thirty minutes per child in the shower.

4. Then they think about getting dressed and getting ready.

5. It takes them another fifteen minutes to figure out what to wear.

In other words, they dawdle. They poke. They drift around the house as if in a daze. Five days a week, they are a well-oiled machine, then on day six, they run out of oil. So how do I keep it filled up? This is what plagues me. If I could just figure this one out, my life would be complete. I will not cure cancer. I will not be president or fight crime. I am even less likely to get the kids to eat asparagus. But THIS, I am sure, can be solved. Right?

Dating Woe or Dating NO?

Today I had a daymare, and yes, I just made that word up. It was a terrible vision of the future, and I saw it all very clearly. There came a time, during my daughter's high school career, that a boy wanted to call her. The boy came up to her and said he had noticed her and wondered if he might call her. I saw her look at him as though he had just caught on fire, then turn and walk away.

Then I saw another possible reality. She said sure, and gave him her number.

I have no idea how I would react to a boy calling my daughter. I see myself eating antacids. The first time some boy comes to the house? I may need to be hospitalized.

I know how to instill fear in my own children. I have no idea how to instill fear into someone else's. And they SHOULD fear me. If a boy were to lay a finger on my child inappropriately… well, let's just say, when I get angry, I morph. My eyes turn red, my horns come out, and I turn green all over. It's not pretty. It's also non-photographical (yeah, I made that word up too), so there isn't any record of it actually happening, but it could. Think leaping tall buildings in a single bound. Think lifting cars like lifting sweat socks. See? It's crazy! I can't even get myself to consider the idea of it.

I have no idea how my mother did it. She was fierce! I didn't date until I was 16. I did get my first "real" kiss at the skating rink in eighth grade (it's OK, she doesn't mind anymore). I rode in cars with boys I met while working at the mall. I dated boys older than me, and boys from other schools, and not once did they meet my parents.

My mind refuses to wrap around the idea of any of this happening to my girls. I'm not old enough, I'm not ready.

I may be old enough to not remember my hair color, but I do remember boys. Boys have hands and ... and ... ideas. I need Depends just thinking about it.

When I was a little girl, my mother told me that a little girl much like me was "taken" as she was walking home in the dark. So it was very important for me to be home BEFORE dark. To this day, I'm still afraid to be out after dark alone. My kids are never out after dark unless they're with me or

another adult. Why? Because as my mother once said, "Kids get taken; it's a dark, scary world." We don't take unnecessary risks.

I'm not sure if boys qualify in that category or not, but look around. Look at the number of teenage pregnancies. Look at the magazine articles that tell stories about the teenage girls that have been killed by boyfriends.

Do I want my daughters to one day find a boy, fall in love, get married, and give me a house full of grandchildren? Of course! But later. Much, much later. After high school, after college, after they are settled into their careers. I think part of the reason divorce rates are so high is that people rush into a life they know nothing about. Before they have even discovered who they are and who they want to be. We have a "why-wait" attitude, when we should have a "don't settle" attitude.

I met my husband my senior year in high school. We went to college, THEN we got married. Of course, then we figured out quickly where babies come from. But I didn't settle. I knew who he was, who he would be, and who I would be with him, before we married. I knew how many cavities he had ever had. I knew every tiny detail I could think to ask. I saw the gene pool. I knew what I was working with. I knew for certain that I could never get through this life without him and that no one else on the planet would ever make me happier. OK, I also knew that no one else on the planet would ever tolerate my antics, but who better than the biggest instigator I knew, to be my partner in life? I want that for them. BUT LATER! MUCH later!

I worry about my younger daughter, too. I have a feeling I'm gonna be busy with her. I have it all planned out. I will have the boy come to the door. Interrogate him intently, find out where they are going, and then my covert operative training will take effect and I will stealthily follow them around town to make sure they go where they said they will. Then I will beat them home and nonchalantly sit down as though I were reading a magazine, until he walks her to the door and she comes inside. But if they stay in the car too long, then I will flash the outside lights. That's what my mom did.

I know what I would like to happen, but I am also realistic. My girls will probably date while in high school. And I may be able to get through this without the Depends. The Tums I'll still need, but it's OK. I know someone who can get them for me, and he delivers.

Beware of Teenagers! NO Dogs Allowed!

I am not a pet person. That is not to say that I dislike pets; I do like them in theory. I like them from a distance. I do not have the time or inclination to spend all my time letting a cat rub all over me, or taking a dog for a walk, nor do I want to clean up after them.

I live in a quiet little neighborhood where the most exciting thing to happen in a decade is the trash truck catching fire one day. That being said, I do not fear for my safety. So I don't need a watchdog. I have two cats, one who has a troubled relationship with a robin, while the other cat has a twin living nearby, so I have to check every night to make sure it's our cat coming in for the night. I should also mention that both cats are old and fat and couldn't summon the energy to attack, even if it were necessary. What I do have, however, are teenagers!

Should anyone feel the desire to come into my yard uninvited — well, or even invited — they may be greeted by a cat rubbing against their legs, which is actually a silent plea to be taken away from this crazy house, or there may be a knock-down, drag-out fight between two teenage girls happening.

They could be fighting because one looked at the other wrong, or said something to provoke the other one, which opens a special can of "whoop arse." I should explain that my husband and I do not fight. We have never laid a hand on the other in a malicious way, nor have we ever beat on our children. Where this sister-on-sister violence came from is a mystery.

As an only child, I cannot fathom what two girls, who are lucky enough to have each other as siblings and friends, would have to fight about. We do have satellite television, but the parental controls are set up, and we monitor all television and Internet activity. I would hope that if they had suddenly become WWF fans and decided to try out their moves, or wanted to try their hand at roller derby, I would understand where these ideas stem from.

My childhood addiction to family shows such as "Full House" and "Family Ties" apparently gave me unrealistic expect-ations as to what a real family is supposed to be like. Not once do I remember DJ ripping out Stephanie's hair. I also seem to remember all the Cosby kids being very fond of each other, and if they did get into arguments, I don't remember one of them getting the other on the floor for a good beating. So what on earth has happened here?

My children do not see prime time television, while their counterparts are watching "Grey's Anatomy" or "CSI," mine watch Disney channel or Nickelodeon. While their counterparts are on Facebook and MySpace, mine are on Poptropica or on Dan Schneider's blog, finding out how he gets ideas to create shows such as "iCarly." They also have a fondness for searching YouTube to watch shows from my generation, such as "Silver Spoons." (Ricky Schroder! He was sooo dreamy. I was president of his fan club, you know.) They also spend time on MuggleNet, learning about all things Harry Potter, and then go to Club Penguin. These are not activities to spur on violence, right?

My husband says that his sisters fought all the time. It's normal, he says. I do not remember reading this in the manual. I would like to have had some warning that this would happen. It wouldn't have changed anything, but perhaps at least knowing what was coming would have been a way to prepare for the inevitable. I try to tell other younger mothers what is to come. I say that they are in the easy era with small children; the hard part is coming. Usually, they don't like hearing this. But I do this for their own good. As I said, I would have liked to have had time to prepare. I don't know what else to do to help them.

I had friends over yesterday. While they were walking in the door, the girls were in the other room, and very discreetly decided to rip each other a new one. My spy (AKA, my son) came to tell me they were fighting. In the time it took me to get into the appropriate room, one of them had fled to her bedroom. The other one remained lying on the floor holding her head, where the other had yanked on her hair. She told me to let her lay there to die (oh, the drama). The provocation? She said it was her sister who got scared during a movie and not her. Imagine—the nerve! I went upstairs and offered to take the bully outside so she could pick on someone her own size. She didn't take me up on my offer. By the end of the day, they were best friends and had a sleepover in the oldest girl's room.

Keeping up with the constant switching of gears is exhausting! This is why we have pharmacies. This may also be why some animals eat their young. This is why I read books. When I read about Nazi Germany or even some teenager's love triangle between a vampire and a werewolf (go Team Edward), breaking up my girls' arguments doesn't seem like such a difficult problem to have. Also, it's much easier to ignore them and let them work on solving their problems themselves if I'm wrapped up in a book.

So let this be my public service announcement: Beware of teenagers! To get through this difficult time, get a good book, take two Tylenol, and call me in the morning, for this too shall pass.

And So It Begins...

My daughter stayed home from school recently for two days because she was ill. When she was feeling better, she had some homework to make up.

When I asked her what I should write about on my blog, she said, "Your experience with me the last couple days, of course." Two of my children have had a stomach thing. A 24-48 hour bug, which makes them toss their cookies till the cookie jar is dry, if you catch my meaning. So my experience with them has been keeping them in bed. Bringing them Sprite and crackers. Then we moved on to toast.

Today, you wouldn't know they had been sick. They were up and ready for school and on their way, right on time. I spent the day cleaning the house top to bottom, spraying Lysol on every conceivable surface.

Lysol is my friend. I have wondered if you could have a form of Lysol for people. I know, I know — it's called medication. But think how much easier it would be, if you could just spray them down and all the virus and bacteria (and baggage) they were carrying just went away. They wouldn't be contagious anymore, and everyone could just get on with it. (Of course, I appreciate convenience. I use frozen mashed potatoes and

have never cut up a whole chicken in my life. Why should I? You can buy it already cut, chopped, or diced. It just makes life easier. It also brings your meals to the table considerably faster.)

This evening, my daughter spent some time getting all of her homework caught up, and then had some tests to study for. One of these tests was a vocabulary test, which she asked me to help her study for. The following is how that exchange went.

Me: What does "retentive" mean?

Daughter: It means to tent again, because re means again.

Me, sighing heavily and putting my head on the table (reading the sentence in the book to help her): The sentence is, "A retentive memory is a great asset for any actor, especially one who performs on stage."

Daughter: Yeah, I wish I had one.

Me: Me too, maybe then you could remember what retentive means. What does premonition mean?

Daughter: Uh? Consequence?

Me: NO!

[While she thinks about this, I'll tell you what I think. I have a premonition that she is not going to pass this test if she doesn't figure this out.]

Me: Premonition. Pre- means to come before. Be-FORE. Forewarning. Pre-before-forewarning. Premonition-pre-before... forewarning.

Then, with my inability to keep on task, simply because I said "fore" several times, I had to look up the Gettysburg Address, so we could go into what four score and seven years ago meant. Then we started talking about the D.C. trip we took last school year, and the Ford Theatre.

You see where she gets it.

Lately, I've been looking for a job. This week, I put in an application at one of the elementary schools in our district. Then I took a test on Facebook that said that I should be an elementary school teacher.

I suppose we should be thanking God at this point that it didn't say I should be a high school teacher, as the previous play-by-play shows you how good I'd be at teaching a high school student. If this child fails this test, I only have myself to blame. Actually, my child is very bright and gets grades I could only dream of having in school. She gets that from her father. She also gets her affinity for jeans and t-shirts from him, but that's a subject for another time.

I can only imagine what kind of teacher I would be. I have a friend who said she thought I'd be a good one. This friend doesn't know me well. All she sees is that I like kids, and some of them seem to like me all right. Although the children she sees me with every other week are preschoolers. It's really not that difficult to look like a rock star to a preschooler. They are very easily bribed. You just give them some Goldfish crackers and water, and they are set. They play, smile and pretty much behave like angels, until the parents arrive to pick them up. It's not rocket science.

High school, however, is a completely different animal. Here I am, fourteen, almost fifteen years after having my first child, and I'm just now getting the hang of the little kids. I haven't a clue what I'm doing with teenagers.

I suppose all I really need to do is talk about Facebook and Twitter, and know all my texting jargon. If you can speak the language, I figure you are at least in the game. I told my high schooler that when I was in high school, I took a shorthand class. She had no idea what I was talking about. I told her it was like texting, only instead of using ttyl or brb, it basically looks like squiggles. Texting jargon is easier to learn. I don't remember any shorthand now, even though at one time, I could take it 60 words per minute. It must be a lost art, like writing letters.

We will be waiting by the phone until someone decides I could do a good job working with hormonal pre-teens at the last stage before junior high. To my credit, I have gotten two of the three through that school, pretty well unscathed. If that job doesn't work out, I figure I can ask around and see if I can get hired to clean houses. I've been cleaning my own since infinity, so I think I could handle that.

Just don't ask me to work in food service. That wouldn't be good for anyone involved. When my children got their flu bug, they were convinced it was my cooking and that they had food poisoning. It couldn't possibly be the flu. Of course, it was the flu, as none of the rest of us got sick and we ate the same things. This was good news, as I had considered the possibility myself.

College Letters Already?

When we first moved to Pleasantville, getting our mail from the post office (since it isn't delivered this far out) was one of the fun things to do. Now, it rarely crosses my mind; I might go get it once a week.

This morning as I was eating my breakfast, I went through the mail. As you can imagine, it was full of the usual: bills, bills, and more bills. But wait! What's this? A letter from a college to my daughter? But she's only a freshman. Does it really begin this early? She opened it and it said they wanted her to

visit the school. She then said, "Why? I've already been there on class trips. I've seen the school."

It certainly sounded like a recruitment letter, even listing a special phone number to call if you wanted to come to visit the campus. We are only nine weeks into her freshman year and already we are getting mail from colleges? She doesn't even own a class ring yet! (A source of contention in our house, as EVERYONE already ordered theirs.)

It's not that I haven't thought about the fact that, in three short years, she will actively be searching for the establishment to suit her needs. And it's not as though we don't have things in place financially. But college letters already? She hasn't even gotten her first phone call from a boy yet. She hasn't given one thought to a prom yet. She still fights me to go to camp!

How on earth are we supposed to think about her going to college? The college in question is only about 20 minutes away. She could live at home. She'd have to, for what it costs to go there. I'm pretty certain I could send her to her dream college (Brown) for what it costs to go our local place.

Let's not put the cart before the horse, here, people. I get it. Really, I do. She is growing up, and like it or not, she is going to leave and start her life without me.

I sit here thinking of how my children and I are connected. I imagine three cords stretching, one to each of them. The youngest one's still pretty close, but just starting to pull away, as he realizes that he is getting a bit too big to be so attached to me. One is moving farther away as she starts looking around at junior high, looking forward to high school, but still wanting to stay within reach. Lastly, the oldest one, pulling farther still. Stretching and pulling and looking towards what's after high school, college, and moving on with her life.

They all hurt; the oldest one a little more than the other two. Because what comes after the stretching of that one, comes the complete sever: the place where she can make it on her own without any help from me. Although I know that is what my job as mom has been, preparing her for life, I can't help but think how much easier and comfortable it all was before now. Before the college letter and class rings were the magnetic alphabet letters and the smiles at toddler jokes.

The more I think about it, I think she would do well at the local college. It's close to home. She would be required to take Bible classes. This is the kid who recently said to me in the car, "Hey mom, you know how in the New Testament it's all about Jesus?"

To which I replied, "Yes?"

She said, "Well, do you think Jewish people don't believe in Jesus because they want less to read?"

When I finally stopped laughing, I did try to explain it all to her, to the best of my knowledge.

Maybe a Christian college would be a good thing for her. Maybe by then, she will be outgoing enough to ask the questions she never asked in church. If nothing else, she would provide her professors with some comedic relief.

NO Boys Allowed

In our house we have a no-boys-allowed policy. I have instilled in my children a desire to dream big; therefore, since not one boy at their school looks like Taylor Lautner (or any other Hollywood star), they aren't really interested. We have also stressed the importance of an education and how boys will only distract from the ultimate prize (being an educated, well-rounded woman who can take care of herself).

So I find it a little disturbing that there are junior high girls that are so obsessed with having a boyfriend that it seems to be their only focus. Don't get me wrong. I absolutely think it's a healthy part of growing up for boys and girls to be noticing each other at this age. I do NOT, however, find it appropriate for these children who aren't even capable to hold a license to drive a car (much less find a matching pair of socks half the time without assistance), to be "dating" and spending time fondling each other, while their parents sit idly by doing nothing about it.

Taking pictures of these children and reminiscing about young love isn't going to keep these kids from going too far and getting pregnant before they are old enough to even apply to a college. In my mind, it doesn't compute. These kids have barely embarked on puberty and are still trying to figure out what THAT entails.

Every coming-of-age movie I ever saw where parents were included in the film, the father always tells the daughter something like this: "Now, listen to me. A boy will tell you lots of things. Like how pretty you are, how they can't live without you, how if you loved them, you would show them your stuff. This next part is the most important part: it's ALL a lie. Any boy, anywhere on this planet, will tell you anything they think will work to get themselves into 'The Promised Land.' I was once a boy myself and I know."

Does anyone remember getting that talk? I got that talk, most likely from a TV dad, but I still remember it. When my daughters are 16 and they can demonstrate that they know how to use a can of Mace, I will let them start dating. But only after I meet the boy and they pass a simple interview, of course. I figure if the boy fears me just enough, he won't try anything that might cause him harm.

What Do You WANT From Me?

As a parent, I hear the following quite a bit: "What do you want from me?" Sound familiar? I also say them a lot, but I thought I'd share my answers to that question.

1. I want you to accept the possibility that I may actually know what I'm talking about.

2. I want you to understand that in five years, it will not matter who you sat beside at lunch, but it will matter what grades you got, because that will affect what college you get into, thus affecting the course of your life.

3. I want you to realize that those who are your real friends will never say anything behind your back that they wouldn't say to your face.

4. I want you to know that your real friends will not be nice to you in church on Sunday and then treat you like a leper on Monday at school.

5. I want you to do homework the moment you get in the door so you can unwind later, and prepare yourself for tomorrow.

6. I want you to know that I will go to bat for you any day of the week and twice on Sunday, but if you are wrong, I will tell you, and you will be responsible for making it right.

7. I want you to dream of all the possibilities life has to offer and I want to ensure you that the only person who can hold you back is yourself.

8. I want you to respect the fact that while I am not a rocket scientist, I am your mother, and therefore, should be respected as such. I also want you to know that mother trumps friends, always.

9. I want you to know that if your friends decide to jump off a bridge and ask you to jump, too, you best bring an extra rope, because if I can't talk you out of it, I'm jumping with you.

Project Conversation

After coming home one evening, I saw my daughter with a project board on the kitchen counter. Apparently, her homework was to decorate a board, and when I came in, she was trying to fix what her father had "helped" with; a mess was the result. The following is the conversation that transpired.

Me: You need to always have me help you with the board. Dad is for research, not for decoration. You do not ask a man who doesn't pick out his own ties to help you decorate a board.

Daphne: What are you yelling at me for? You married him! Why did you marry him, anyway?

Me: Because he has got the nicest butt I ever saw, and the very first time he kissed me I felt it all the way down to my toes. That, my dear child, is fate! He is my counterpart. The other half of everything I ever longed to be.

Daphne: EEEWWW MOM! Gross! You do not tell your child about their dad's butt! It's disgusting!

Me: Then don't ask me questions that have answers you don't want to hear!

Driving

My daughter is almost finished with driver's training. She has driven with her father and two of my friends. Yesterday, we made it all the way from our house to the gas station in town before I made her pull over. Did she do something horrifically wrong? No. I had a panic attack. She is my oldest child, my first child to be learning to drive.

I am not handling it well... obviously.

My daughter is growing up. In many ways I can see that she is. In other ways, I still see her as this little girl. She still watches Disney Channel and Nickelodeon. OK, so she watches "Glee" and "Degrassi" too, but she can sing the theme song to "Phineas and Ferb." I'm just saying, it's not really a stretch for me to look at this girl who rarely wears makeup, doesn't party, and wants to marry Daniel Radcliffe, and still see my little girl. On the flip side, I haven't had to wake her in the morning since elementary school. She gets up with an alarm and gets herself ready. She babysits her brother and even cleans up the house. She studies hard and does her best in school. She is a great kid. I'm lucky.

My other daughter isn't too far behind her, either. They are nineteen months apart. They loved to wear dresses, even if it wasn't a special occasion. They loved "The Big Comfy Couch" and "Bear in the Big Blue House." We took them to see "Blue's Clues Live" at least three times.

Now they watch movies with kids with flying brooms and "vegetarian" vampires, and I can't help but wonder how we got here so fast. Soon, they will be off on their next adventures, and I won't be there to experience it with them. I have always been there. Perhaps that is where the problem lies. Driving is one step closer to the next adventure, and I won't be invited.

I had to apologize to her yesterday. It is entirely my fault. I give her mixed messages all the time. I want her to grow up, I want her to spread her wings and fly. I want to see what God has planned for her. At the same time, I hold her so tightly that she can't get her wings out. She didn't ride a bike without training wheels until third grade. Why does she need to drive at sixteen? Shouldn't she wait until eighteen, you know, when I'm more prepared?

When I was a child, I was scared to go down the slide on my little swing set in the backyard. I still don't like heights. But when you get a bit bigger, the little slide doesn't seem so big anymore. I think maybe driving will be the same way. Eventually, it won't seem like such a big deal. After all, it will be nice to have another driver in the house. Someone to go grab milk or some other ingredient you forgot at the store while you're preparing dinner. Someone to drive me around.

I only drive out of necessity. At sixteen, I remember loving it and thinking it was such freedom. I don't know where or when the change took place. Maybe around the time that I became the taxi mom, when I was never home. Don't get me wrong; I am thankful for the opportunities that have been given to my children, and that I was able to take them places, and to be there for them. But at one time, we were gone every night. Those days are no more, and I am thankful. For as much as I enjoy watching them in their activities, I love being home with them together even more. Especially now, when our time is limited, and they will be going off to college in a blink.

Driving. Driving to school, driving to the movies, driving to the mall, driving to a friend's house, driving to college, driving... away. It's funny how as a mother, your perspective changes from moment to moment. I have told them that they have to go away to college because I have plans for their rooms, and yet when I think of their rooms not being occupied every night, it makes me sad.

I know it will be fine. God has a plan for each of my children. I am so excited to see what it is. I just have to loosen my grip. I have to let go. I have to trust in God and His plan. After all, I know they aren't really mine to begin with; they belong to God. You can only hold a hand if you open yours to accept another into the fold. How can God hold my hand to walk me through this, if my hands are holding my children so tight that they can't go and fulfill God's plan? The answer is: He can't. Fortunately, God is patient with me. Every once in a while, I do get the message.

Maybe next time we drive with her, I will ride in the back seat while my husband sits in the front seat. I'm a work in progress. I'll make my way to the front seat ... eventually. She did say she was going to need to be able to drive so she can drop me off at the nursing home. And that her brother is going to be paying for that. I was informed of this about the time I had her pull over into the gas station parking lot. I have no idea how she thinks her almost forty-year-old mother is going to the nursing home anytime soon.

I think I will stick around awhile, though. Her driving may come in handy. I do have places I would like to go that she can take me to. And I know a great pharmacist. Maybe there is a patch I could get to keep me calm while I'm in the car with her.

The Eavesdropper

My oldest is an eavesdropper. It is almost impossible for me to have a telephone conversation without her interrupting. She seems to think that she needs to be included in my discussions, for whatever reason. She is going to be sixteen, so we are not talking about a six-year-old. She listens as she is doing her homework, then gives her input into my conversations. I will tell the person I am speaking to what she says, and it becomes a game. Then she gets mad at me for repeating what she says. So you would think that she would be the one least likely to want me to write about her, when in fact, she gives me so much material, she feels like the star of every post. She loves it.

I read somewhere once, "God gives us teenagers so we won't be so sad when they leave." I have very mixed feelings about this. On the one hand, I can totally relate at times. My son is counting down the days until his eighth grade year, when his two older sisters will both be in college and he will have the place (and us) to himself. I will admit that there are days when I count alongside him. I also wonder what life will be like when the girls have gone to college. Mostly when I think about them leaving, I feel sick. As though a piece of me will be gone, and I will spend all my time trying to find it.

You know that feeling when you've lost something that's important to you? In college, I had a small pin on my coat that had belonged to my great-grandmother. It fell off my coat one day, and I looked everywhere for it. I finally found it in the street, where it had been run over by a car. I was sick about it. Or the feeling when you realize that you are going to be late to pick up your kids from school, and they will be waiting there?

I realize they have to grow up. I also appreciate, on some days with my teenagers, why God gave us pharmacies and chocolate. Raising teenagers is not for the fainthearted. My friend read a book once that told her that if you don't make your kids mad at you at least once a day, you aren't doing your job. This made me feel slightly better; apparently, I'm an overachiever. (It's a gift, really.)

But the expectations I place on them are unreasonable. At least, in the society we are raising them in, where most adults are more concerned with hurting a child's feelings, rather than teaching them right from wrong, I expect my children to work hard at school. I expect good grades, and that they do their own work. I expect them to pick up after themselves and to do their chores. If they do not, I keep the money I would have paid them for myself and have a nice cappuccino with a

friend. I expect them to be respectful of each other, those around them, and of themselves. I expect them to use appropriate language. I expect them to dream and to plan for their futures. I expect them to not settle for less.

I am still working on my expectations for myself. I think mostly I'm going to have to expect that when the time comes, I will let them go. I will let them spread their wings and fly off to wherever and whatever God has planned for them. But one thing I will do when I drop that oldest one off at college someday: warn the roommate to take her calls in private.

Man Business

When my oldest turns sixteen, she will be eligible to begin dating. Well, we're hoping that it's more like thinking about dating. She currently is in love with a boy that is not within her reach—Daniel Radcliffe. He is not only seven years her senior, but has a girlfriend, and is a huge movie star. So she's probably not on his radar.

I completely understand a teenage girl being fond of someone famous. When I was in junior high, I was going to marry Ricky Schroder. I then moved on to Kirk Cameron, then Rob Lowe. I made my rounds.

She has read all of the Harry Potter books, and seen every movie that he has been in. The only things she has not seen are "Equus" and "How To Succeed In Business Without Really Trying," the two plays he has been in. In "Equus," well, he shows his man parts. While she would like to see EVERYTHING Mr. Radcliffe is in, we did have to have a conversation about this.

(Note: Having any kind of "talk" with one of my daughters makes me wish for the time when the hardest part of my job was finding hats, shoes, and binkies to match all of their clothes. It also makes me want to eat chocolate and shop for pretty shoes.)

Our talk went a bit like this:

D: I could look it up on YouTube and watch it there.

Me: You are not going to watch "Equus."

D: Why not? I want to see everything that he has been in.

Me: Because he shows his man parts in that play, and you don't need to see them.

D: So?

Me: So? SO? You don't see the problem here?

D: Not really.

Me: Listen. If and when you marry that boy, you can look at his man business all day, every day. I won't even stop you. But you are not even 16 years old, so you will not be looking at anyone's man business, including his, even though he has chosen to bare himself to the world. AND if you do marry him, you would be the last one to have seen it. You will have people coming up to you asking you about his man parts. Where is the mystery in that?

D: Really? You had to go there? OK … I don't think we need to discuss this anymore.

Me: Thank you. Now go watch "Degrassi" and stay off YouTube.

Perhaps someday she will leave and work in the entertainment industry as a director, like she hopes to do. But if it doesn't work out with Daniel, she's keeping her options open … that Taylor kid from the "Twilight" movies also has a place on her bedroom wall.

Aunt Flo Follies: Who REALLY Pays the "Monthly Bill"?

When I was a kid, when referring to our monthly period, we always said that "Aunt Flo had come for a visit." She is the worst aunt ever, by the way, and at our house, she comes three times a month.

She (Aunt Flo) just barges in here unannounced, like she owns the place. She is rude and disrespectful. She makes such a mess. The girls hate her. I tell them it's not nice to hate, but what can I do? If my friend (Midol) comes to visit at the same time, they are much happier and the aunt is easier to deal with. I even redecorated to throw her off track, but it didn't work.

I have heard an urban myth that when women live together, their cycles tend to align. In the last four years, the stars have only aligned for this to happen once in our house. Which is why it may be an urban myth. Not even two of us get the same week. So we have the pre-, the during, and the post-, for three women, which is really just a lead-in to the pre- for someone else. It never ends... ever. Three females, with two males living in one house, with cycles all out of line. I have told my friends that if you want to pray for someone, pray for the men who live in my house. I am sure there are worse fates. However, when the monthly bill arrives in our house, EVERYONE pays for it.

I have convinced myself that I should buy stock in Midol. She is a great friend. She keeps all of our sanities in check. That, along with the numerous cappuccino drinks, gives me the energy to keep up with it all. Of course, the only thing that is doing for me is adding to the ever-expanding waistline. This does nothing at all to help with my body image. Especially when you're so bloated that you're carrying more water weight than Shamu.

I sometimes think back those early years with my aunt. In the year or so prior to her first visit, I remember being excited and ready to be a woman. Of course, I also remember thinking, after her first visit, perhaps it might be better to be able to write my name in the snow. At least that wouldn't be painful or as messy. My mother's best friend had brought me a big box full of necessities. I was prepared, in that sense, anyway. Unfortunately, the box full of products did not include Midol or Pamprin. The box also didn't include a heating pad, or even a warning label as to what all this entailed.

When my first child received her first "visit," she was devastated. Far from the excitement I had. She wanted to know how long this thing was going to last. I said "Well... for about a week every month, till you are maybe fifty or so."

She was furious. She said, "Seriously? I ask you a simple question and you can't even give me a real answer!"

I then had to remind her of my age and that mine still came every month. When she realized I was serious, she was even more devastated than before.

I have to say, even with all the drawbacks that come with the monthly bill, I rather enjoy being a woman. The wardrobe is so much better. Just in the shoe department alone, I would never make it as a man. That, and they pick a hairstyle and go with it, forever.

I guess while the payment of the monthly bill can be high, it's all worth it in the end. If nothing else, it is certainly an exercise in patience, and learning to be accepting of people no matter what their mood (or yours) may be. As I tell my kids, you may not be able to control what is happening to your body, but you can control how you react to it.

If all women everywhere acted like crazy people when they had their "special" time, it would be the end of the human race. I tell my girls that women all over the world get through "that time of the month" without incident. If they didn't, they would either kill each other, or the men would do away with them in frustration, and civilization as we know it would come to an end. Then the men would all just go back to hunting, and put a pig on the spit for dinner. (Incidentally, the words pig, spit, and dinner just don't belong in the same sentence.) I tell the girls they have GOT to get it together, if only for the evolution of dinner variety.

Which is why I believe prayer, Midol, and the occasional cappuccino, to be the best remedy for Aunt Flo's visits.

Eve, Apples, and PMS

I really don't like snakes. I don't like spiders, I don't like lizards, I don't want a mouse, a guinea pig, a hamster, or any other rodent. But mostly, snakes just really tick me off.

The fact is that I'm at a moment-by-moment relationship with God. I try to get through my day a moment at a time, without blowing my stack, even if I encounter snakes. This is important, as I have teenage girls. If ever anyone should be medicated, it would be the parents of teenagers.

Don't get me wrong. I LOVE my teenage girls. But I can think of few things that can make you tempted to lose it like breaking up a fight between teenage girls who know better. Or trying to teach your teenager to drive.

In the movie "Date Night," they discuss a book. In that book, the girl gets her father and her brother to get into an argument so she can go off into the desert to "menstruate in peace." In peace. If only. Can you imagine if we were able to go off into our rooms and sit with our remotes, a pile of chick flicks, a stack of books we have intended to catch up on, a bottle of Midol, and some bon-bons? That's not feasible, but it's fun to dream.

As adults, we tend to have selective memories of our own childhoods. For example, I remember being a very good child. I was top notch. Why, in my memory, there may not have ever been a blessing of such a fantastic child outside Jesus himself. I didn't run with the wrong crowd. I didn't smoke, drink, or "get around," as they say. No phone calls were ever made to my mother about me getting into trouble at school.

Now, if I take my hip boots off for a moment and wade out of the garbage I just fed you, I will tell the truth. I was a brat. I was a spoiled kid of divorced parents who both tried to buy my love. There, I said it. I wanted for very little. I had a big mouth and I, on many occasions, would open mouth and insert foot, thereby getting myself into a world of hurt. I may not have done any really bad things, but I was bad in my own right. I was a PMS queen. As punishment, I can only assume, I now have TWO PMS queens.

I blame Eve for this. Actually, I blame the snake (hence my disdain for them). I'm sure the apple looked good. I'm no stranger to temptation, especially food. I have often said that the way to my heart is through my stomach. I have lost weight in the past, and said, "I will never put this back on again. I am going to keep it off and prove I can do it." Then I rediscover my love of ice cream, and pizza, and all those things that taste good but will kill a new-found love of fitness.

I imagine that Garden, filled with all sorts of delightful things to eat, the choices too numerous to count. Then the serpent comes and points out the shiny apples. "Don't they look good? Surely, one bite won't hurt anything." Oh, but it did. And now we get to experience the hurt every month, over an apple. (I have always wondered if it was a Delicious?)

Disobedience is a killer. Raising my own children, I expect to be obeyed. I will not tolerate disrespect. It is the biggest pet peeve I have. Just yesterday, my younger daughter was teasing her sister and called her dumb. The sister responded by dumping a plate of chips on her sister's head. I had to force myself to calm down so I could speak to the elder sister. I found out when I spoke to her about it, and then spoke to them both, they were able to forgive each other a lot easier than had I just lost it and yelled.

We know that God knew, of course, what had happened in the Garden. I wonder if He ever just looks at us and says, "Really? Have we not learned from this mistake yet?" Eve was, after all, human. She had an apple and then had Adam try it. That one mistake resulted in the PMS cycle of turbulence in our home today.

At the end of my life, I will still have no idea what mistake I might have made that changed an outcome for someone else. But through it all, our God shows grace and mercy to his children. I think perhaps it is a test. With all the hormone surges and pain that comes upon women during that time, how can we show grace? How can we learn to live and walk with our Father anyway?

From what I've learned in my journey thus far, I think only when we are broken can we fully see; only when trials arise, do we look. So when the teenagers start in next, I will think about Eve. Maybe I will give the girls an apple and tell them a story of one woman who made a mistake, and then I will try my hand at showing them grace and mercy. Instead of laying down my wrath for their indiscretions. Then, maybe some time when I'm having one of those days (and I'm looking for chocolate), I will be handed an apple. And I will remember.

Not So-Hollywood Holidays

Halloween, Orange, and Other Nonsense

If you were to ask me what holiday I like least, the answer would always be Halloween. I like candy, but I can buy candy at the store any time of the year, and avoid passing it out to strangers. I just do not understand why it's acceptable to dress up like the living dead and walk through the streets of town scaring small children and well … me. Plus, what is with the knocking on strangers' doors and begging for food? These trick-or-treaters aren't starving, and if you try to give them something healthy, like an apple, they are likely to toilet paper your house. The decorations are just as bad. I spend half my year trying to get spider webs off my porch — why on earth would I go buy artificial ones to decorate my house on purpose?

When I was a little girl, I wanted to go trick or treating like all of the other little kids. My mother would take me only to the houses she knew. In kindergarten, I was invited to a little boy's Halloween party. As I liked this little boy very much, my mother took me to the party. We had no sooner started up the walk to the door when someone in a scary costume jumped out at us. It scared me to death. To this day, I remember nothing else about the party. I don't even remember if I stayed for it or not. After that, my mother would take me out trick or treating through the neighborhoods, but it soon lost its appeal.

Another problem is the colors. Orange and black? Really? I own one orange shirt that I break out in October. It doesn't have a pumpkin or any other foolishness on it. I do not wear clothing with holiday embellishments of any kind; not Christmas trees, Easter bunnies, or pumpkins, because I am over the age of eight. Orange is for pumpkins. Put it with black and I may have a physical reaction. My gag reflex is only so strong. I even have to give myself pep talks to buy anything orange for anyone in my family. Why anyone would want to look like a pumpkin is beyond me. As Elle Woods on "Legally Blonde" would tell you, "Whoever said that orange is the new pink is seriously disturbed."

I have sucked it up and taken the kids trick or treating since they were babies. Mostly because they like it and they usually share the chocolate with me. We only go to our neighbors' houses, and then we go to our church for the community party they have every year. It feels a little less wrong when we go to the church. I also do not allow any scary costumes.

One year, my husband and I dressed up with the girls. It was because I had such a great idea for our costumes that it seemed a waste not to do it. I was pregnant with our son at the time; due the next month, actually. I wore an old bridesmaid's dress, which I had worn while pregnant previously. I put on my great-grandmother's tiara, and went as a pregnant cheerleader. My husband wore his Purdue basketball jersey and went as the ball player that got me pregnant. Funny, right? A couple of 30-year-olds dressing up like teenagers. We did have a good time and we got our own candy that year because some of the houses got our joke.

As that baby I was pregnant for is going on nine now, and is the only one of our kids who is still trick or treating, after he's decided it's too childish for him, I will probably miss the excitement on his face when he gets a regular-sized candy bar instead of a fun-sized one. It's not my favorite holiday, but at least it's one time of year that I'm not required to decorate.

I can't help but think maybe there are some good parts to the holiday after all. If, for no other reason, the food is pretty good. Every year our town has a pumpkin walk, and the church has a chicken and noodle dinner. On the pumpkin walk, you can get homemade kettle corn. And everybody likes that.

With Great Thanks

In the month of November, I know several people who have listed every day, as their Facebook status, one thing they are thankful for. I participated in this activity in years past. This year, however, as I look at my life, there isn't enough server space on Facebook to cover what I'm thankful for. You see, I am very happy. With great thankfulness comes great happiness. As a child, I was given plenty of material things, but longed for the relationships that I wouldn't experience until nearly adulthood. When I married, I was given the gift of creating the family that I had longed for as a child.

I was taught to be thankful for whatever I was given. And I was always thankful, even for the things that I didn't necessarily want or need. At any given time during my childhood, I could take you through my room and tell you who had given me everything I owned. It is entirely possible that I could do that now, including things belonging to other members of my family. But what I'm most thankful for as an adult aren't things.

So sit down and grab a hot chocolate.

--I am most thankful for a God who forgives. Who delivers, who gives, and takes away.
--I am thankful for the God who delivered me from the pit that I held residence in for so long, that it didn't seem possible to get out.
--I am thankful for the One who gives me strength and the love that I am certain I don't deserve, but gives it in abundance anyway.
--I am thankful for my husband. He is my love. He embodies everything I could ever hope for in a man. He is kind, loving, reassuring, nurturing, and quite possibly, the strongest man on earth. It takes a strong man (in body and spirit) to tolerate being married to me. He is the best father to our children and a great provider for our family. He is my partner in this thing we call life.
--I am thankful for my oldest child. She is smart and beautiful, inside and out. She likes to come across as strong and mature.

But she is kind and loving and accepting, too. She doesn't like change but she adapts, and usually, will admit when she is wrong. When I get sad for any reason, she is there to bring the tissues. She is a great daughter and a great big sister.
I couldn't be prouder of the young lady she is becoming. We like to say that she was the prototype. We made our mistakes with her, but she is amazing anyway.
--I am thankful for my middle child. She is truly a wonder. She has come so far. She didn't speak until she was four, and now she performs on stage. She is a miracle. She is her own person, and definitely doesn't do what everyone else is doing. She is strong and smart, and full of life. I am amazed by all she has been able to accomplish.
--I am thankful for my son. He was our little surprise. He is so smart, and has the greatest smile. He truly cares about people. He always wants to include everyone and strives to do the right thing. He is the great peacemaker, in a house full of high-strung emotional women. He makes me smile daily, and I look forward to seeing what God has planned for him. There isn't a child I know that has more faith than he does.
--I am thankful for all of my family. My grandmother, who gave me the gift of the love of reading. My parents, who at least got together long enough to give me life. Every relative who has given of their time and love to help form the person I would become.
--I am thankful for the time I had with my mother, even though it didn't seem long enough.
--I am thankful that I didn't get the mother-in-law that all the jokes come from. God blessed me in that area especially, because I couldn't have asked for a better one. She is loving and funny, and I enjoy every bit of time I get to spend with her. In fact, I am thankful for all of my in-laws. I don't even refer to them as such. They are just my family; no in-laws or out-laws about it.

--I am thankful for my friends. They are all gifted in so many areas, and I learn something new from just being around them. My friend Christi, who is a sister to me in every way except biologically. I'm still holding out hope that my son will marry one of her daughters. She is always there to lift me up or talk me down, as the situation requires. She also isn't afraid to tell me when I'm being an idiot, which I love about her. (This happens more than you would think.) She is, along with each and every one of my friends, a great treasure in my life.
--I am thankful for my home. I understand what a gift this is, as there are many in the world who do not have one. I have been blessed beyond measure to have a home to call my own, filled with the people I love most.
--I am thankful for food to eat. I am never left hungry, which I am so very thankful for. I understand what a blessing this is and I appreciate this blessing of abundance.
--I am thankful for clothes and shoes. I am thankful also that I can share some of these things with my daughters. It makes it even more fun when you wear the same size shoes.
--I am thankful for the ability to see. Not just so I can get around daily, but so I can look around and see all of the beauty of God's creations. It also helps with my love of reading and writing.
--I am thankful for time. Time to spend with my children, my family, my friends. The time I've been given and time I may have left. As none of us know how much we have been given, I'm thankful for each second of it.
--I am thankful for hugs. I love hugs. Especially from my kids.
--I am thankful for heating and cooling.
--I am thankful for electrical appliances. I don't have to use a washboard to do my laundry and I rarely have to do dishes by hand. I also am able to keep my perishables cool. I don't have to cook over an open fire. (Imagine how bad my cooking would be then.)

--I am thankful for windows.
--I am thankful for the ability to cuddle on a couch and watch a movie with my kids.
--I am thankful for my car. I'm scared of horses, so a horse and buggy wouldn't work for me. I would never have made it in the old days. And as the cats rarely do what I say, I'm thinking a thousand-pound animal is even less likely to follow my instructions.
--I'm thankful for my cats. They aren't really too demanding. They are great at keeping your feet warm and (knock on wood) I haven't seen a mouse in some time.
--I am thankful for our children's school and teachers. Without them, they would never learn that "new math." And without them, I wouldn't have the school breaks to look forward to, and may take for granted having my children home with me.

This isn't everything, of course. There is so much more. Things like blankets, and chocolate, and Midol. Things like indoor plumbing, and clean water, and cleaning supplies. It would take forever to list them all and I still couldn't cover the depth of my thankfulness and gratitude.

This Thanksgiving, I challenge you to look around. How are you living your life? Are you living it with a heart of thankfulness? I know there is pain and hurt in the world. I have suffered plenty, but if I lived my life dwelling on what has been instead of what is yet to be, it would be no life at all.

I choose to live a life of thanksgiving. A life full of possibilities, of imagination, of giving praises and glory to God who makes it all possible. Won't you join me?

The Christmas List for People Without a List

The annual Christmas shopping trip with our Sunday school class is this week. I am so excited I'm about to burst. I love the opportunity to get together with these wonderful women. Plus, it is great to get a jump on the holiday shopping. I even had a dream that I had forgotten about going, and went to work. I was at work when it occurred to me that it was 9:30 a.m. and I wasn't supposed to be there; I was supposed to be in a car with my friends. I woke up very distraught, until I realized what day it was.

I put a post on Facebook to tell my friends and family that I needed their Christmas lists by Thursday of this week, as the first round of shopping was to take place. I informed them that if I didn't have a list, I would buy what I thought they needed.

This got all sorts of ideas flowing through my head for gifts I could give people that they may or may not want.

1. I could order M&Ms in Christmas colors with the person's name on them and make a collage of their face on cardboard. Who doesn't love a homemade gift?

2. I could have a star named for them. To my knowledge, none of them have a telescope to find their star in the night sky, but they would have a cool piece of paper to frame.

3. I could buy nail polish in various colors and make a chart for which color to wear for each of their moods. Pink for perky, blue for sad or blue, black for mad, red for feisty. That way, the general public would know what they were dealing with. They could pass out pocket charts for their friends and family.

4. I could get them a notepad so they could write the script for what they want people to say to them. Then they would always hear what they want, instead of the truth, or in some cases, what they think they hear. Give a copy to the person they are having a conversation with and everyone walks away without getting mad. (You know people like this, right?)

5. I could get your kid a drum set and, oops, I forgot to get you earplugs.

6. I could buy days of the week underwear. Then you are assured to never wear the same pair twice in a row. (This is especially good for kids. Plus, they learn the days of the week and how to read them.)

7. I could get you frog socks. Not just any frog socks, but the ones that actually make your legs look like frog legs.

8. I could pull what my kids sometimes do to me, which is to get you what I want, then ask to borrow it. Then I would just take over said item, leaving you with nothing, and I would have just what I want.

9. I could buy you cleaning items. Laundry soap, dusting supplies, dish soap, etc. Because what everyone wants are things they can actually use, right? Or you could take it as a hint that I think you need to clean your house.

10. I could rescue an animal at the pound and put a big red bow around its neck, and write up a card that says, "This animal told me it wanted to come live with you. Enjoy!"

As you can see, if you have specific things you want for Christmas, it's a good idea to give me a list. You have no idea what I might come up with. But whatever I get for anyone, I will be sticking to my budget. I will not go into debt for anyone on my list. Which makes me think maybe I will just get everyone a Dave Ramsey book... or maybe not.

Christmas Cards

I'm not sure if my mother sent out Christmas cards. It is entirely possible that she did without my noticing. I don't remember them being as big of a deal as they are today.

When we were first married, we would go to the store pick up a box of cards and send them out. We tried to pick out a style that was nice, but we didn't really put too much thought into it. The greeting card industry makes millions each year off something that most people read once, then throw away. Unless it's a Christmas card, then it gets used as decor on a door or a wall for a month.

After we had children, we thought it would be nice to include a picture of our kids with the card to show how they were growing. Then it became a family picture. Then it became a family picture card. After all, who doesn't want a picture of the family? Why, it's a gift in itself! I'm sure that all those people who live out of town are curious as to how the children are growing, and old friends love to compare how well they are aging as opposed to us.

It started easily enough. We needed to get a family picture done every year, to show how the kids were growing, and for sentimental reasons. I bought the girls new dresses every year anyway, so they needed their picture taken in them. As time has gone on, it's evolved a bit.

For the last few years, I have resorted to themes in our family pictures. After all, my oldest is in high school, so I have no idea how much longer I'm going to get away with this family picture thing. For me, family picture day has become my Christmas of sorts. For one day each year, everyone looks nice and has a smile on their face, at the same time. That is my joy. Seeing my family happy, even if they have to fake it to get through a picture. Any mother will understand what it takes to pull this off. Especially a parent of a teen.

The first year we did the theme was actually by accident. It was becoming increasingly more difficult to come up with outfits for five people that would look cohesive in a picture.

I was out shopping with a friend saw some hats. Fedoras actually; black with white pinstripes. They were SO cool. I kept going back to them. My friend said she thought I should do something with the hats, but I just couldn't figure it out. Then it hit me. We should all wear black and white. We should be the mafia!

I am not a card-carrying member of the NRA, and had never even let my kids play with toy guns. So I had to go to the dollar store and buy plastic ones for props. That year, our cards said "Merry Christmas from 'The Family.' "

How do you follow that? I had no idea what I had started. So the next year it was "Twilight." Allow me to introduce myself. I am Bella, my hubby Edward, of course. Followed by one daughter as Alice, the other Rosalie, and my son was Jasper. If I hadn't been too old and had I had time, I would have attempted to give birth again so we could have had an Emmett. I also wanted to use the neighbor's German shepherd to play Jacob, but was outvoted. Nevertheless, the photographer we have is a genius, and the "Twas Twilight before Christmas" card was very cool.

This year's theme I actually figured out very early. We have been working on updating and remodeling our home all year. So the theme was easy. Almost too easy, at least one would think. You would think that borrowing five tool belts would be an easy task. It was not. In fact, I didn't get them all until about two days before our pictures. We have also decided not to allow the theme to be leaked until the cards are sent out.

What started out as a simple family picture and Christmas card has now turned into a double-sided, 5X7, full-color picture card. These things aren't cheap. When I say they are a gift in themselves, they truly are. By the time I get done with these things, I can't afford to buy gifts. Then there's the postage. I joke that when I was a kid, all you had to do was whistle for a horse and they would deliver your mail. All it cost you was a drink of water for the driver. While that is a complete exaggeration, it still didn't cost 45 cents to send a card. This doesn't sound like much, until you figure I send out about 50 cards.

I do all of this because, in the back of my mind, I know that soon enough, it will come to an end. In a few years, my oldest will be gone to college. Sure, she'll come home for Christmas, at least the first couple of years. But if she is like her father and I were, the time will come when she comes home for Christmas, and then goes back to her life. She won't have time to come home for pictures. It will be too "lame" for her to participate. She, then her sister, then her brother, will all think they are too old for a family Christmas picture, much less a theme. Then what?

Then I'll be back to those boring boxed cards from the store, and longing for the time when the cards weren't just cards; they were a snapshot in time. They are a small remembrance of days gone by and of how things once were. What will our pictures be like with just the two of us? Just two people who look happy enough, but wish they had those days back, when the kids were around for the family picture?

I do wonder if, once they are grown and married, the Family Christmas Card will mean as much to them as it means to me now. I hope so. But I also can't wait to see what they will come up with for their cards.

Santa: A poem

Tonight is the night that Santa comes to town.
The children are all snug in their beds.
Preparations have been made for when Santa comes around.
The cookies are out, the milk is out too.
But I think of the baby for whom Christmas is named,
All snug in a bed of a manger his parents had made.
The Christmas lights were stars that shone up above,
His family and visitors looking upon him with love.

Happy Birthday my Lord Jesus and I thank you too,
For without you, I wouldn't be here to share your love with my children too.
The love you have shown me all through my life
Is more than I deserve, for that I'll do my best
To show others love and to serve.

Merry Christmas, my dear family and friends.
I hope Saint Nicholas treats you right,
But remember, my dear ones, the reason we celebrate tonight.
For Jesus was born in a manger far away
To bring light to the world and show us a way,
To walk in streets of gold…
And it all started with a manger, filled with hay.

Easter Chocolate

As everyone (except us) gets ready for Easter egg hunts, I'm reminded of a joke a cute little girl told me this week. Why do chickens sit on eggs? Because they don't have chairs.

But it makes me wonder… Where does the Easter Bunny get eggs?

We take our kids on egg hunts, and then we come downstairs on Easter morning to baskets of eggs and prizes because the Easter Bunny has been here. For what? The point of the entire holiday is to celebrate the fact that Christ is risen. Yet every year, we sit our children on a giant rabbit's lap and tell the rabbit on steroids what we want him to bring us.

But hey, what do I know? I'm guilty of telling my kids about the bunny too. And the hyped-up rabbit will make an appearance here this year. After all, who am I to turn down an excuse to buy chocolate?

Don't Ask Me — I Just Live Here

A Pioneer, I am Not

I may be a lot of things, but a pioneer I am not. We were recently under a winter storm warning, so I knew it was going to snow. What I didn't know, until too late, was the magnitude of said snow, and ice. I wasn't too concerned with the prospect of snow, as we have plenty of food to get us through, and don't have places that we need to be. I don't watch the news, and spend most of my time reading books. Then I get all these reports that we need to be prepared for power outages.

I spent my evening looking for the miniscule number of candles that I own. I only own them for decorating purposes, and for when the lights go out. I can't smell them anyway, and the potential fire hazard they hold has always freaked me out. Eventually I found the candles, and the matches, and set them all on the kitchen counter, ready to go. Then it occurred to me that if we have no power, we also have no heat.

"That will be OK," my husband says, "We can layer our clothes, and we have plenty of blankets."

To which my reply, of course, was, "Seriously? You would have us all get naked in the bed, huddled under twenty-seven blankets, using body heat to keep warm?"

After he stopped laughing, he asked, "Why on earth would we need to be naked?"

"Uh, hello, Survival 101? You get naked and use your body heat to survive. If we have no heat in the house, it's no better than being stranded in the car. We are sitting ducks here, kid. Our innate desire to survive will eventually take over. You do know what the temperatures are out there, right?"

This is usually about the point where he just walks off. The middle-aged drama queen has taken over and all reason has left the building. He spent the evening at work. I spent the evening looking for him to come through the door and save us from impending doom. Instead, he was saving the rest of the town from their impending doom by supplying their medications before the storm set in.

I texted him at work, asking if we should consider buying firewood for the fireplace (that we only used once, ten years ago, and don't know how to use now). I explained to him that if we had some firewood, we could cook our food over the open fire, like the pioneers did. I could hear the sarcasm in his text when he responded, "You are going to light a fire, over which to cook food?" I said I was hoping he would light the actual fire when he got home, and then I would become all pioneer woman, and cook wonderful meals with biscuits. We could eat out of tin cups. (In this fantasy, I am also somehow wearing a dress and an apron, and my hair has miraculously grown long enough to be put up in a bun.)

The idea of me cooking over an open fire is ridiculous, to say the least. The irony here is that I'm currently learning to cook more than the five staples we usually eat. Also, I rarely bake, and if I do, it's those pre-formed cookies. The last time I made pre-formed cookies, I burned them. Apparently, there is a rather large difference between 375°F and 325°F. My mind said 375, the instructions, however, said 325. Hence, only one tray of warm moist cookies was the result, with several of the crunchy variety.

When he came home from work, I was snug in my chair with a blanket, a space heater running in the room, watching a movie. I figured I should be as warm as I could, before my habitat became cold and uncomfortable.

We will have to survive (if and when the power goes out) on cereal, chips, and Diet Pepsi. Because I may be a lot of things, like a middle-aged drama queen, but a pioneer I am not.

****

Dear Martha Stuart,

I would like some advice. I have been told that my kitchen isn't very functional. So why not just take the entire thing out? I hate to cook, and I'm not any good at it. Also if it's not functional, why should I bother?

I need some decorating tips. I was thinking (perhaps you should sit down for this) I could rip out all of the kitchen-type things, except for the fridge and microwave, and make one really big family room, as the two rooms are connected. I could give all my dishes and cookware away and use disposable stuff, eliminating the need to do dishes. Plus, if I have my meals delivered from a food service (like a diet program, as I'm getting kinda meaty over here), it's all microwavable anyway. Problem solved. There should be laws against this kind of brilliance!

But how do I incorporate my fridge and microwave into my now massively extravagant family room? Oooooh wait--

I got it, curtains! Like the "Wizard of Oz!" My goodness, I'm a genius!

Not domestically yours,

Heather

****

Redecorating is Hard; Moving is Easier

Let's Either Move to Florida, or Redecorate!

My mother once said I was born old. I joke now that I was born 35 years old. I am well on the other side of 35, and I am pretty sure that in my comfort, I've aged myself an extra 30 years. Unfortunately, however, I do not seem to be getting any more patient with age. And, before I tell you the story you are about to read, I want it known that this was not entirely all my idea.

I should also preface this by saying that I *should* live in Florida. The sunshine. The salty breeze, the warm sand between the toes. But alas, I don't. You see, I'm a Midwest girl. Born and raised. I grew up in a small town, not far from the smaller town that I ended up in. The only difference is the one I live in now isn't riddled with bars, and there's no house-to-house mail delivery.

It's very quaint here. The main street is tree-lined, with a very few businesses. When the sun is just right, I can imagine I am in a different time, or part of the cast on the Andy Griffith show. It is that Mayberry here. There are good schools and it's not too far from decent shopping. We have one stoplight here and the top speed limit in town is 35. It's comfortable; it's home. My children are all in school here. I do volunteer work, I have lunch with friends, and my husband is in the Lions' Club. We're settled.

I just wish this home was a little further to the south.

We have lived here in "Mayberry" for 10 years. Aside from being the last people in the neighborhood to mow our grass, and perhaps the only people who do not have a degree in landscape design, it's been good to us. Our neighbors are nice, and as I said before, the schools are excellent.

My inclination towards Florida began with our vacation there. It was wonderful. No, it was better than that; it was heaven on earth. We went to the beach, we went to Disney World. Even the food tastes better in Florida. But after that vacation, it became clear to me that waiting to move there (like, for retirement) was a crazy idea. We wouldn't enjoy it nearly as much then. If we lived there now, our children would get to go to Disney all the time. Isn't that every child's dream come true?

The only holdup was convincing them that they wanted this dream also. So, even before we came home on vacation, I started in on them.

"Wouldn't it be nice to be able to play volleyball all year long?"

"You know, if we lived in Florida, when you are old enough, your summer job could be at Disney. And I bet if you worked at Disney during high school, they would help pay for college."

"Snow is really heavy to shovel, honey. It would be good for your back to live here."

All to no avail. I tried my arguments for an entire summer. They wouldn't budge! You think childbirth is hard. Try to convince teenagers they want to move away from all their friends.

I went with another angle. We have lived here, like I said, for 10 years. We moved in when the girls were 4 and 2.

Toddlers... with light carpet and white walls. Very quickly, our house looked like a well-used college dorm room. Stains all over the carpets, with the walls painted dark to cover the crayon.

And, you can accumulate a lot in 10 years with three kids. This means, it's not a place conducive to rest and relaxation. So I proposed three options:

Option A: Let's sell this place and leave winters behind — we can move to sunny Florida.

Option B: Let's sell this place, and build again.

Option C. We need to fix up this place so I can relax. Let's redecorate!

So guess which one my husband chose.

I'm pretty sure that it could be argued that I am a failure in my profession as a stay-at-home mom. Decorating and organization is not my strong suit. Need an expert on decorating, cooking edible meals, knowing which cleaning product works best, and getting your whites their whitest? That's not me. If you want to go shopping and pick out clothes or shoes, or you want good book tips, I'm your girl. I clean, I cook things the Schwann's man delivers, I run my kids every which way but loose, and I read. That's my day.

So deciding what colors we should use and how to put it all together was a stretch for me, to put it mildly. I inquired about professional help. In the closest town to us, there is a furniture store that is owned by a decorator. Knowing that it was likely that I could turn our house into something worse than what we were starting out with, my husband agreed to hire someone.

It's not that I don't have good taste. I'm just very eclectic. My styles vary, like my music selection. I could mix modern with Victorian and have nothing be cohesive, or comfortable. I needed someone who could listen to who I was and figure out my style. After a consultation, my style was determined to be funky modern cottage. Isn't that just awesome? As a woman who picks out lipstick by the name alone, this label delighted me.

Her ideas for my living room — now named the "receiving room" — were exactly what I wanted. I did try to tell her that we rarely had visitors. She responded that when my home was something I was proud of, I would be more apt to invite people in. Little did she know, that is not really true. Once we got nice things, I wouldn't want company, because I want to keep it nice. I have a fit if the kids wear shoes in the house, and if you even think of taking food or drink out of the kitchen, my head spins around.

The process began, and it was exciting. We chose a paint color, we emptied rooms, filled nail holes, and repainted. With the painting done, we ordered the flooring (goodbye stained carpet, hello hardwood). All the old furniture was put into storage to await a sale. We ordered new furniture.

It was October.

Some of you may know already what I didn't know, going into this project. Furniture can take 10 weeks to come in. TEN weeks! Not ten *days*, ten weeks. And apparently this is normal. We live in an age of computers. Ten weeks is a long time to get furniture that is more than likely sitting in a warehouse somewhere, waiting to be transported. In ten weeks of being pregnant, I was almost done with morning sickness.

If you were to ask my family what my strongest suit is, they would not tell you patience. They wouldn't tell you cooking, or baking, or organization either, but by far, patience is lacking in my temperament. Perhaps it's an only-child personality trait that I just can't ditch.

The decorator was wonderful. She came up with some great ideas. What she didn't come up with is a timely manner of getting things in.

****

Letters That I Wrote But Never Sent

Dear Furniture Store,

As I am aware that furniture doesn't grow on trees (or does it, since it is made from wood?), I am pretty sure you aren't waiting for the trees to grow, so you can chop them down to build me a couple of bookcases. I am also pretty sure that you aren't growing cotton in your backyard to spin so you can make me a couple of pillows. So I am a little confused as to why it takes 10 weeks to get these things in.

Are they being made by Spanish monks in the middle of an island, from special trees that can be chopped only at their maturity, then handmade by the monks with hand tools? Are there Amish ladies in the woods spinning cotton by hand, working by candlelight to make these pillows? Are they being hand-carried across the country, or sent on donkey carts?

I'm thinking that, in this day and age, there is a factory somewhere that cranks out about 100 of these things a day. And is there not a UPS or FedEx near the factory that could ship these things out in a timely manner? I'm running a little short on patience. So, furniture store, thank you for selling me the perfect decor and then withholding it from me for eons so that I can appreciate it more when it comes in.

Signed,
Disgruntled, Yet Very Patient Client.

****

Dear Furniture Store,

I have tried not to write this letter all day, but unfortunately can no longer control my sarcasm. While I am ecstatic that the Spanish monks who were building my bookcases finally brought them to fruition and that you are now holding them hostage in your store till Thursday, I am a little disappointed with the fact that it takes nearly eight weeks for decorative couch pillows.

 If I had been aware that the company you ordered from was going to take this long, I would have gone to the store to buy white pillows and some fabric paint and make them myself. Or perhaps I could have grown the cotton, spun the fabric, and made the pillows myself in that amount of time.

Perhaps in the future, you should warn customers that if they want pillows, they would do just as well to go to their local discount store and choose something else, if they want them before menopause hits. Also, they could probably get 10 pillows for what you are charging for two smallish pillows that probably weigh less than 1 pound together.

So thank you, lovely furniture store, for beautiful furniture that I have had to wait eons for, that hopefully lasts for 10 years or more. That will be the next time I redecorate, and then I will order everything from eBay so I can get it before I need a nursing home.

Sincerely yours,
A VERY Patient Customer.

****

Our decorator also lacked understanding of what the word budget means. The next lesson I learned was that everything is more expensive than what you plan. After living with hand-me-downs for so many years, buying all new things to furnish a room turned my formerly excited husband into a reluctant husband.

"It's going to cost how much?"

Ah, money. Why must you be such a bother? I read a book series not long ago in which there was no money. In fact, the things you wanted or needed were just given to you. There was a hole in the wall that would just spout out the thing that you ordered. I think the author was a genius. If we could live this way, wouldn't life be easier?

We only used the decorator for two rooms, and then I took over, with a little help from my friends. This went much more smoothly. I had paid attention and learned a lot. I learned to use neutral colors, and then add in accents of color. I also learned that ordering furniture from JCPenney.com takes a lot less time than 10 weeks. In fact, you can order an entire roomful of furniture for the cost of one sofa from a professional. The process didn't take nearly as long and it turned out very nice. Our home became our home; a calming, restful place to come home to.

We were done. Life was good! My reluctant husband loved the results and was very happy.

Then, phase 2 began. Just as I was beginning to relax and enjoy the fruits of our labor, my husband looked at me and said, "You know, if we're ever going to add on, we should do it now. Our oldest will be driving before we know it, and we are going to need the extra driveway space. What do you think?"

I'll tell you what I thought. "This man I married is nuts. We are finally all done. I don't want to start over. I want to rest. I want to take a vacation."

What I said to him was this: "1) You figure out how we can possibly afford it, 2) You get someone we can trust to do it, 3) You don't give me any grief over decorating the new room that we will gain by adding on the garage and then you have my blessing. When it's finished, I will NOT have an empty room, and I will have it done in a timely manner."

Perhaps now would be a good time to introduce myself. I am the one who had a C-section because my first child wouldn't come out ONE day early. I am the one who had to switch majors in college because my program was wait-listing me for another year that I didn't have time for. I am the one who waited 10 years to decorate her house into something that didn't belong in "PeeWee's Play House." I am the one who is habitually now at least 15 minutes late for almost everything. Welcome to my world.

One year later from the big "let's remodel what we already have" suggestion, we were a carpet strip and a garage weather-stripping away from being done, and were hit with a freak hailstorm. A contractor told me that the missing shingles, the holes in my brand-new siding, a mangled screen door, and dents in my gutters and downspouts, along with missing parts of my fence, amounted to about $20,000 in damage. He suggested I call my insurance company. My anniversary trip to Hawaii, which turned into a garage, was now going to cost me my deductible to fix.

I am tired. I think Florida still sounds nice. Tomorrow's forecast for Orlando is sunny and 83°. Tomorrow's forecast for here is just sunny and 66°. If we could pick the entire town up and move it to Florida, I could then use something other than a snow blower in my newly enlarged driveway.

More construction is in my future. More waiting for normalcy. I scarcely remember what that's like anymore. My home is my castle still; it's just a little beat up at present.

I would be lying if I said that I didn't love my "new" house. However, the process of the great re-make wasn't an easy one. Over the course of 15 years of marriage, and having children, we accumulated a LOT. Getting rid of a great deal of it, and using just what was needed, has calmed me immensely. I no longer feel it's best to be away from home, because it's simpler now to get it all cleaned up, and this calms me. Before, there was just SO much that it overwhelmed me, to the point that I would have rather moved. So I'm very grateful for the lessons we learned in this process.

This is what I know now: 1) Deliveries only happen when you are painting in another room. It also helps if it is a holiday. 2) It doesn't matter if they have a factory full of furniture, you will get yours when they get good and ready to send it. 3) Washable fabrics are your friend. 4) And patience is a virtue, but delivery is divine!

Observations from the stairwell while I was painting:

1. How on earth did I paint this before?

2. I know I'm old, but is it possible I'm shrinking already?

3. I've been painting for a week and I haven't lost a pound, maybe I'm doing this wrong.

4. I think we should order pizza for dinner.

5. I wonder if I can talk him into letting me paint the laundry room so I can get out of cooking another meal.

6. Spidey powers would come in handy right about now. I wonder if the resident spider that usually eludes me could get that corner for me; at least then he would be useful.

7. If I reach real high, do you think my arms will get longer, so my long-sleeve sweaters will fit better?

8. No, it doesn't smell like paint in here, it's like that "new car smell." It smells like new walls.

9. At least my nails are getting painted.

10. Too bad the paint costs so much. If it cost less, maybe I could have hired someone to do this for me.

You Do Have A Man To Build That, Right?

In our quest to get our home the way I've always dreamed it to be, I have spent more time in home improvement stores than I care to remember. The new item on the to-do list is to build new shed doors.

As soon as Christmas is over, I'm ready to be done with the excesses of the tree and all other decor involved. Last winter, while trying to get the Christmas tree into the shed and out of my house, I ripped one of the doors off of the shed. My shed is ten years old, and the doors were already starting to dissolve in that way they do, with years of weather, and animals trying to pry their way in and out. So when we went traipsing around the yard carrying the tree to the shed, I was not in the mood for the door to be stuck. In my frustration, I used every ounce of strength I had, and ripped an entire door off its hinges. So I decided to build new doors.

Yes, me, not my husband, not a contractor, just little ol' me. The reason for this is that I do not like being told that one of the aforementioned men must take care of this rather simple repair. After all, how difficult should it be, really?

I went to the home improvement store in town and asked for the wood, and had them cut it to the right size. I figured that's the hard part. I know how to use the drill, and I can put the pieces together.

When discussing with the gentleman helping me that I wasn't sure about brackets, I said, "Well, I'm sorry, I don't know the answer to that question. This is what happens when you send a woman to do a man's work."

This statement, followed by my little chuckle, then prompted him to say, "You do have someone who is going to do this for you, right?"

I said that I did have a husband and that he would probably do the work. But I still didn't know what brackets to get. I said I would just come back for them later. The look of relief on his face is what prompted the following.

When I got home, I got the drill out and started putting the doors together. I figured that all I needed now were the six new brackets, some screws, and a lock to hold the doors shut. After I put it all together, I thought about making a sign for the doors: "Doors put together by a woman, feel free to gawk in awe and wonder at your leisure."

I think there are plenty of women in the world today that can follow simple instructions on how to put things together. Even if said instructions are given or written by a man. In our home, we usually put projects together side-by-side. Someone has to read the instructions, after all. And all things being fair, he is better at the things that require more muscle.

The next day, as my husband left for work, I told him that I would have the shed doors done when he got home. He chuckled. I think he gets a kick out of my willingness to attempt things, particularly if someone has said they are things I can't do.

I went back to the home improvement store, and picked out brackets and a lock for my new shed doors. When I got home,

I got to work. I had already fought with getting the doors all put together the day before, so my thinking was that the actual hanging of the doors shouldn't be too difficult. I measured and installed the brackets to the door first, and then I was ready to hang them onto the shed. I did have to get them lined up and to do that, it turns out, I had to balance it on my foot on one end. I got them hung up, and examined my work. Not bad. The only part my husband had to help me with was the closer for the doors.

My doors turned out pretty good. I impressed myself. Now, if I get them painted before I need to make new ones again, is another story altogether.

Outdoors: A/C or Automatic Comfort?

All my life I thought A/C stood for air conditioning. There was a time when I would have thought that A/C stood for A.C. Slater from "Saved by the Bell," but those days are gone, too. Now I believe that A/C stands for automatic comfort.

In the last week, the temperatures outside were well into the nineties. We noticed the first time we tried to turn on the central air that it wasn't cooling the air. We called for service, and waited a week for someone to take a look. Meanwhile, the temperature inside rose with the temperature outside. My thermostat inside only goes up to ninety. It was straining at the top of the gauge.

We purchased 10-inch box fans for each of the children to have by their bedside, and put a larger fan in our room. Then a friend brought us another fan, which also went into our room.

I started envisioning us as pioneers. While I do know that there are people all over the world who do not have air conditioning, we have been blessed with it for quite some time. If we were brave enough, we could sleep outside in the open.

Then I figured it would be easier just to be creative, staying cool until we could get the AC unit fixed.

Idea #1. Keep large towels in a cooler, and wear those around in the house all day. No one comes to our house anyway, so no one would see us. My husband didn't think this would work. First, they would get drippy and could warp the hardwood floors. Also, he didn't want anyone to sit on the furniture, for fear of ruining that, too.

Idea #2. I need to lose a few pounds anyway. I'll sweat off the pounds by sitting in an overheated house.

Idea #3. Maybe we could keep buckets by the front and back doors. When company came, they could bring their own ice and sit in the ice buckets to keep cool.

The entire situation was frustrating, and everyone was a bit on edge, but it was still a bit funny to me. I spend the entire winter being cold. My hands are cold, my feet are cold, and although our heat does work, I am usually under a blanket. One of the perks (and there are many) of being married to my husband is that he is very warm-blooded. He is often warm and doesn't mind my cold hands and feet as it cools him off, while warming me at the same time. The poor man was miserable in the heat.

The night before the air conditioning unit was replaced, it was hot, and my son had baseball practice. I was in the house waiting to go out to dinner, when I felt my skin boiling from the inside out. I put my suit on and jumped in the pool; I'm pretty sure steam rose from the water.

We then went out to dinner, in a lovely air-conditioned restaurant. To top it off, we had ice cream. That evening,

coming back home was a shock to our now-cool bodies.
So we got creative with sleeping arrangements. Our son slept in our room, on the floor, with the big fans. The girls shared a room and had three smaller fans surrounding them.

Through it all, I couldn't help but think how lucky we were. While it was inconvenient not to have A/C and be in automatic comfort, we did have soft beds to sleep on. We had screens in our windows to let in the night air. We had fans to at least move the hot air around, and most importantly, we had each other.

No one can commiserate with you better than those enduring with you. I don't think we can be defined by the things that disrupt our lives. The washer goes out; the dryer goes out or eats all the socks; the A/C goes out; even the one winter that the heat didn't work; or the summer my mom died, and my world seemed to flip upside down.

Trials come, trials go. The trick is in the surviving. And while I've had my share of meltdowns, I think it's still best to sit back and enjoy the ride. Because surviving in style, acknowledging the grace of God in everything you encounter, is so much better.

Neurotic Much?

A Whole Lot about Me...Quirky Not Crazy

It's a little embarrassing, but it's been brought to my attention that I may be, well... quirky. There, I said it. I have these things about me that are just a little different. Actually, they are relatively new developments as I get older.

1. I absolutely refuse to go to Wal-Mart alone after dark. I just won't do it. There is nothing I need that badly that won't wait until morning. Out of milk? Guess I'll have to go to the

corner mart and pay double in the morning for breakfast, but I am not going to Wal-Mart after dark alone. I believe that is when all the crazy people are out. If someone wants to mug you, it will be at night. I prefer to be in my house after dark. No midnight strolls through a park for me. The sun is set; I'm in for the night. Unless I'm already out, and of course, there are others with me.

2. I will not drive in the snow, or during a thunderstorm. There is nowhere I need to be that badly that I need to go out in bad weather. Unless one of the children is somewhere and I need to get to them, it's not happening. If I was meant to drive in the snow, God would have had the snow fall everywhere but the road. Plus, I don't have four-wheel drive. Probably a lame excuse… but it's all I have.

3. Interstates. Why do I need six lanes? No one is going the speed limit but me. People fly down that road at unnatural speeds. Seriously, it's just scary. Why are they in such a hurry to get where they are going? I'm pretty sure wherever they are going will still be there when they get there, if they go at a rational pace. I hate these roads. I never know which lane I'm supposed to be in, and forget about switching lanes if you get into the wrong one—the speed demons are not going to let you switch lanes. If I absolutely must take an interstate to go somewhere, I try to carpool, so I won't have to drive. I also offer to buy lunch if they will do the driving. Or I have them meet me somewhere, so we eliminate the need to go on such a crazy stretch of road.

4. It gives me chills to think about making a meatloaf. I have attempted meatloaf before, and it never turns out. Also, it makes me gag to put my hands in meat, to mix it up. I'm not certain that is how meat was meant to be prepared. I know it's a popular entrée, and people tell me I'm crazy because they love meatloaf, so I should too. I do like it, if other people

prepare it. But it is by no means a favorite. If a friend or family member made it for me, I would eat it. I wouldn't dream of ordering it at a restaurant.

5. When I go to a restaurant and order an ice water or an iced tea, I will always order it with lemon. Not because I want to squeeze it into my drink, but because it looks pretty on the glass.

6. I make friends with salespeople if I think I'm going to see them more than once. My friend pointed this one out to me. I never really thought about it. I suppose it's true. I'm friends with my Schwann's man. I'm not sure if that counts though, as I've known him since he was a kid. Also, my favorite store used to be Maurice's. I knew all the salespeople by name and they knew me when I walked in the door. Not because I spent so much in there, although I bought clothes for myself and my teenage daughters there, but mostly because I would go in there and talk to them. Even if I wasn't going to buy anything, if I was in the area, I would stop in and visit. None of them work there anymore, and now my new favorite store is Kohl's because they have better sales and, I'm old. I've crossed over the age limit for Maurice's.

I think all of these things about me are pretty reasonable. All I know is this: God made me, and He is crazy about me. He loves me, and if I need to make changes in my life, He will let me know.

I guess it's interesting to have things pointed out to you about yourself. Things that you never really thought about. How boring would it be if we were all the same? I purposely surround myself with people I can learn from.

Ode to Smell

I can't smell. Don't ask me why. I think it's a side effect from having kids. Before I was pregnant, I could smell. When I was pregnant, I smelled everything. Have the kids, and boom, I can't smell a thing. Unless it's terribly strong and/or my nose is in it, I can't smell it.

When I go to Bath and Body Works, I have to take a friend because I cannot tell the difference between any of their stuff. It all smells the same to me. In fact, if left to my own devices, I will just pick the color of packaging that I like best. Sometimes this works out, sometimes not so much.

Usually, I will tell the salesperson — if I think they won't steer me wrong — to point me in the direction of the clean scents. I don't want to smell musky, or like a field of flowers. I want to smell clean, with a hint of something fresh.

Going to Bath and Body Works with my friend Christi is the most fun. When you go to a place like that and you can't smell, it tends to irritate the help. They can't really sell me on the newest scent, if I don't have someone I trust with me. Christi is a good go-between. She speaks Heather, and she also speaks retail. I speak retail too, but definitely not as fluently, so I can be a bit exasperating to them. Mostly to those who lack a sense of humor, or take their mall jobs entirely too seriously. (If your job hinges on me buying the newest fragrance, I'll just apologize now.) Christi once told me a story in the middle of a Bath and Body Works that had me doubled over in laughter, and we even had a touch-and-go moment there where I thought I'd wet myself from laughing so hard. I didn't, but it was close. I foresee having to wear Depends as we get older. And the two of us will probably get kicked out of a store at some point.

I do buy scented soaps, and I buy scented room fresheners. I cannot smell them, but I buy them. My friend thinks it's funny that I do this. She says that she understands that I want to make sure things smell good, but how would I know if it didn't? She has a point.

I'm your best pick for changing diapers, because chances are, I'm not going to smell it. However, I can still see, so it's not like I won't be repulsed by what I find.

The diaper phenomenon first came to my attention after I had my first child. I was in the habit of checking her diaper every hour or so while at home, but when out visiting others, I wouldn't do it all the time. I would be sitting around, talking to the family, and my mother-in-law or someone else would gently point out that the baby "needed a change." Nine times out of ten, I would be the one holding her at the time, or at least sitting next to the one holding her, and I didn't smell a thing. It got to be a joke. I started telling them that whoever smelled it, changed it. I got out of changing a lot of diapers that way. My lack of smell did turn out to be a pretty nice perk then.

I sometimes have phantom smells. Once, shortly after we moved into our home, I was playing with the kids and watching TV, when suddenly I was sure that I smelled natural gas. I was just sure that I smelled it, and I knew I needed to get the kids out of the house. Even the children assured me that they didn't smell anything. But I grabbed the cordless phone, and took the kids outside to call my husband. I told him that I smelled gas and asked him what I should do. Who do you call for that?

He said, "Honey, you can't possibly smell gas. We don't have gas appliances. Well, unless we eat chili. We are totally electric. It's fine. Go back inside."

When my mother and grandmother were still alive, they wore perfumes all the time. At times though, they would wear too much. Especially grandma. I'm sure it was because she couldn't smell it if she didn't put enough on. It was overpowering at times. I don't want to do that to people, especially if I can't smell it. I think you shouldn't be able to smell anything anyone's wearing, unless you are close enough to hug them. Which limits the people who will smell it anyway. Do we want total strangers coming up to us and telling us we smell — good or bad? I don't think so.

Ah Inventions… or, Why Can't I Ever Find What I'm Looking For?

If you will ask my friend Christi, she will attest that I have led her on more than one wild goose chase. I'm not a very good shopping companion. In college, we would go to Wal-Mart together and I would fill my cart with things, as would she, only I would put my things back before checking out. She would be in line, paying, incredibly frustrated. I suppose sometimes for me, it's just the walking around and looking at things I like. I don't necessarily want to bring stuff home. If I bring it home, it takes up space, or I have to clean it.

But sometimes I get an idea in my head of something I need; something we really must find, because it would be great to have. Then we search. I believe the first time this occurred was for my oldest child's second or third birthday. She was crazy about "The Big Comfy Couch." I thought, "How great would it be to have a birthday party with that theme?" So we went in search at a number of party places and department stores to find the gear. You know, plates, napkins, cups. Only we didn't find anything. Not one Big Comfy Couch item.

So Christi, who is incredibly patient, turns to me finally and says, "Heather, this is something you've seen before, right? You know it exists, right?"

And I said, "Well, I haven't actually seen the stuff anywhere. But it is a great idea! They SHOULD have it, right?"

"Seriously? You have had me running all over town for something you've NEVER seen before?"

"Yep."

To my credit, I did not completely make it up. Finally, another friend introduced me to a catalog called Birthday Express, and I found everything I needed in there. That is the worst instance I can recall.

Of course, sometimes the quests turn on me. Like the time my husband said he'd "be the happiest man alive if he could get a PlayStation 2 for Christmas." That year, I searched online and in four different cities to find it.

I got the same response each time from salespeople: "You will never find it, you know. We have a waiting list!" Of course, I didn't know any of that. I know nothing about video games. (I didn't even have an Atari when I was a kid. When I was a kid, we went outside to play, and when we watched TV, we got 3, sometimes 4, channels.) All I knew was that my husband wanted one and I should do what I could to get it for him.

So at the last stop, I went up to a salesperson and said, "Please sir, you would help me to make my husband a very happy man on Christmas, if you would only allow me to buy a PlayStation 2."

To which he replied, "Well, you are in luck! We gave people until a certain date to pick them up, and the person who had their name on this one, didn't pick it up! I happen to have one I can sell you." JOY!

My husband was very excited to open it up. And then he played it five whole times! He seemed to remember after that,

that he was a grown man who worked for a living, so the kids gladly took it over for him.

I've been in search of a cord. No, I've never seen it before. No, I have no idea if it exists. What I need is a cord that, at one end has the HDMI plug, and the other end has the cable connector. I also needed a cord with the HDMI at one end and the three-headed component plug at the other end; the ones that plug into the all the accessories for a TV. They always have the three-headed component end cords, but not enough plugs for them at the back of the TV. However, all the new TVs have the HDMI ports. My thinking here is that I can plug everything into my new TV, if I only have these kinds of cords. Sounds logical, right?

Today my claim will be, "Please sir, I need these cords…"

Is It Really Gray Hair or Is It White Gold?

Today I did my morning ritual of checking my hair for grays. I know I am in need of a color job, so I check daily to see what new surprises await me. It occurred to me though, that they don't look gray at all. More like silver. "That's not silver at all," I hear whispered to me, "it's white gold!"

Perhaps you don't have conversations with God in the morning while getting ready, but I do. In fact, some of our best conversations happen in the restroom, because sometimes it's the only place I can go without interruptions. I believe that if He has something to say to me, it's best if I can give my full attention.

Of course, the distractions are mostly my own doing. For example, I don't do my Bible study at the kitchen table, because all I will be able to focus on is the dirty dishes in the sink. If I try to work at my desk, the computer is there, and I check email, or I see the stacks of pictures waiting to go into albums. So, I do my Bible study in my bedroom, where there isn't anything to keep me from my time with God.

Doing my morning hair inspection, I thought about how I was blonde as a child. As with all the children in our family, our hair gets gradually darker as we get older. Mine, however, got very dark after I had my second child. It was so dark that my mother asked me what I was putting in my hair to make it look like that, and to stop immediately. I was twenty-five at the time, and had never put color in my hair, as I explained to her. She suggested that perhaps it was time that I started. This began a decade-long relationship between me and various hair colors. The way I figured it, if it was always changing, I would never have to hear anyone say that perhaps it was time to try something new.

It occurred to me, with a little prodding from God, how it was that I came to earn my "sparklers." I've been married for almost 16 years now. We have two teenage daughters and an eight-year-old son (who is, quite possibly, too brilliant for his own good). My children are more valuable to me than the finest of gold or the greatest of treasures. I believe that's how God sees us as well. He gave me these treasures of HIS to take care of. Perhaps instead of thinking of them as gray hairs that are troublesome, I should think of them as white gold—a sort of badge of honor.

Of course, I'm proud of my badges of honor. But I'm pretty sure that God will be OK with keeping them just between Him, me, and the hairdresser. After all, some gifts we give and/or are given, are best done in secret.

I'm still covering up the white gold, even if I'm proud of what they represent, since there is no need to make others jealous.

Ya Gotta Have Friends — and Chocolate

Adventures with Linus the Cat

In our house we have two adults, two teenagers, a child, a geriatric cat (Gabby), and a crazy long-haired, black cat with a white patch on his neck, named Linus. Linus enjoys sleeping on the white couch. I think he feels he'll get noticed more if he is there. His other favorite places to sleep include the following: on my bed, under my bed, the top of the stairs, the middle of the stairs, on either of the recliners, and on my lap.

I once gave my cats a bowl of milk. They looked at it as if it were poison. I ended up throwing it out. However, if the kids leave their milk out in the morning, Linus feels it's his duty to jump onto the counter and see what the problem is. He sticks his face into (usually) the child-size Tupperware cup, spilling it all over the table and floor. *New rule: If you do not finish your milk, you must put it into the fridge to be finished later, or put it in the sink.

Just this week, while I was watching TV, I heard a noise. I turned around and found Linus standing on the kitchen island. I looked at him and said, "Really? Get down!" He got down. Then, after the program was over, I was turning off the lights that weren't being used, and where did I find Linus?

He was standing on top of the washing machine, of course. Isn't that where all cats hang out in their down time, between sleeping where you want to sit down, and eating? This was a first. It was made even more curious, as the lid was open, so it took some balancing on his part. Nothing was in the washer at the time. I wonder what he could have been looking for. I do have hopes that he will learn how to do the laundry, as it is a job that I haven't delegated. It would make up for the fact that he leaves black fur on the white couch.

Last night, after everyone was in bed and I was turning all the lights off and heading upstairs, Linus was asleep in the recliner. To his benefit, I did wake him up. Then I went up to bed. He followed. Which leads us to our nightly adventure.

Each night the cats come up to bed with us. There are plenty of places to sleep downstairs, but of course, they like to sleep near people. Linus, however, thinks that it is his job, nay, his duty, to be with us all the time as Guard Cat. So they both sleep at the top of the stairs, or in the doorway of our room, or our son's room, where they can "stand at post."

When I roll over, or seem to be too comfortable, Linus comes to the rescue. He makes himself comfortable 1) at my feet, or 2) in the space right behind my legs, somehow positioning himself between me and the edge of the bed, which then makes it impossible for me to move. If one of the children move to roll over, or get up to use the restroom, Linus will get up, watch them, walk them back to bed, then go back to his post.

Our other cat, Gabby, just goes along with these escapades out of a feeling of obligation. She is old. She is tired; she just wants to eat, sleep, and be left alone. She is the cat version of a grumpy old lady and she will nip at you if you aren't moving fast enough to feed her.

I am my mother's daughter. My mother hated cats. I have never hated cats, I simply preferred dogs. As the kids say, these cats are not just cats, they are members of our family. Linus is definitely like one of the kids. He reminds me a lot of my kids, actually. When he wants my attention, he wants all of it. When he wants to be left alone, well, I leave him alone, because he's a cat. If he was a child, I would only pretend to leave him alone, while sneakily trying to find out why he wanted to be alone.

But he doesn't ask for much. I feed him and he gives me his undying love and devotion. How many people can you say that about? Maybe that's why we get along so well. We speak the same language.

****

Heather: Hey.

Cousin Misty: Hey Lady!

Heather: I need you to tell me if I'm funny. I also need you to tell me not to ever try and do my own nails again.

Misty: You know I think you are funny. I always do my own nails.

Heather: Yeah well I stink at it. I need professional help. Toes I can do. Fingers not so much.

Misty: Have your husband paint them.

Heather: No thanks. He would paint my whole finger.

Misty: Oh come on, he's artistic right?

Heather: No he's scientific. I understand it has an i-c at the end like artistic, but the two should never be confused.

****

The Theater Loves Me .... Sorta

My two youngest children, who are part of a local theater production of "Willy Wonka," are very excited, and so are the rest of us. This is the first time they have participated in the civic theater, so we know nothing about procedure, or even any of the people there.

Tonight I did learn something, though. Apparently, the length of time it takes me to feel comfortable in the theater around virtual strangers is equivalent to two auditions and one full read-through. Tonight was the second rehearsal, and I was talking to people as though we were long-lost friends. At times they looked at me as though I were the long-lost crazy friend whose phone number they'd "lost" long ago… but friends nonetheless.

I think it's possible, given that I'm normally very reserved around people I don't really know, that I was just so excited to have some adults to talk to, I got a little carried away. Other adults do not adapt that quickly with people they hadn't laid eyes on before last week.

The upside to all of this—besides that they will all be trying not to sit in my general area, because anyone who sits near me might have my arm thrown over one of their shoulders—is that I will at least be known for something.

It could be worse, for sure. I could be the overbearing typical "stage parent," or I could be the indifferent parent that acts like they don't want to be there and that it is a waste of my time to even show up. Nope, not me. I'm the parent who thinks we are all new besties and wants to volunteer for sets or props or whatever else the director once said that they may need help with.

The theater is full of crazy people; I should fit right in!

Pretty Food Lovers, Unite

Hello Starbucks! Have we met? Cappuccino or Latté?

My mother drank coffee. Well, sort of. She would drink instant Folgers or Maxwell House coffee, straight up—no cream, no sugar. She had it at every meal. I tried it once, and decided I did not like coffee. I could never see the draw. But one day, when I was visiting with a neighbor of mine, she asked me if I wanted some coffee. I politely declined and explained that I didn't care for coffee. To which she replied that I would like it the way she made it. As it turns out, I do like coffee, as long as I can't taste the coffee. Or rather, I like all the really fattening things that go into the coffee drinks to make them consumable.

There is something to be said for a tall, skinny, Milky Way latté, and all of it is good. Let me introduce you to some friends of mine. They are named sugar, mocha, caramel, milk, cream, and pretty much anything you can dump into a coffee to hide the fact that coffee is my friend.

What I did not learn, however, was how to order these delightful drinks when out and about.

Recently while I was out running errands, I decided to stop at a local bookstore and use a gift certificate I had received for Christmas. It was good for a free cappuccino or latté. I perused the menu and attempted to place my order. I say attempted, because I don't actually know how to order the things I want to get.

How you should probably order at Starbucks: "I would like a tall, nonfat, sugar free, cinnamon dolce cappuccino, no whip, extra cinnamon."

How I order at Starbucks:

Me: Yes, give me something not too fattening that is warm and tastes good, please.

Worker: OK, so you want a skinny?

Me: Yes, I want to be skinny!

Worker: What size?

Me: Oh, give me a medium, I guess. (holds hands up to show the size I want)

Worker (rolling eyes): What flavor? We have skinny cappuccinos in Mocha, Carmel, Dolce, and Hazelnut.

Me: Hmm… they all sound so good. What do you recommend?

Worker (now thinking that I should go to McDonald's where I can get coffee without all the choices): Well, ma'am, the dolce is cinnamon, and is very good if you like that, or you could go with mocha if you like chocolate. That is always a safe bet.

Me: Can you mix them?

Worker (now with red face, ready to quit and get a job at McDonald's where life is easier): Sure, ma'am, what would you like to mix?

Me: Hm... I don't know. What do you recommend?

(Worker starts shooting steam out of his ears, and I get frightened.)

Me: OK, OK, give me a mocha and caramel, uh, mix.

Worker: OK, so that's a grande skinny mocha caramel cappuccino.

Me: Wow, it sounds so fancy when you say it like that! Thanks!

I have a friend who works at the local Starbucks. I love it when she is working, because I can go in there and not need to know how to order. I just tell her to surprise me. Of course, this makes me sound to the other customers as though I were adventurous. But my friend knows that I really have no idea what I'm doing at the coffee counter.

If my mother could only see me now, driving through Starbucks with my gift card. Buying instant coffee singles and flavored creams so when my gift card runs out, I can still get my fix. What would the woman who raised me, who used to drink actual coffee, think of the child who grew up saying, "How on earth can you drink that? It is so gross!" I think if she were still here she would say what I say and what my friend Christi says: I am not a coffee drinker; I'm a dessert-in-a-warm-mug drinker.

A friend and I once went to a restaurant for breakfast and I ordered one of my favorites, which was served with whipped cream and a straw. When she saw this, she cracked up. She said, "THAT is NOT coffee, that is dessert." I have to admit, it did look a bit like a dessert, but if it has coffee in it, it still counts as a coffee, right?

The movie "Kicking and Screaming" with Will Ferrell is a family favorite. While the critics didn't give it high marks, our family gives it several thumbs up. We quote it on a regular basis. In the movie, Will Ferrell is coaching his son's soccer team. He is going up against his own dad, who is a coach on a different team. His dad's next door neighbor is Mike Ditka, whom he enlists to help him coach his team. At one point, Mike Ditka tells him to calm down and have some coffee.

Will's character says, "I don't like coffee, it's a vaso-constrictor."

Mike tells him, "Coffee is the lifeblood that fuels the dreams of champions."

Of course, then Will's character goes to a coffee shop to order his first cup of coffee. He informs the guy at the counter that he is new to coffee and wonders if you can "mix half of the regular version with half of the decaffeinated version, or is that just too weird to think about?"

That would be me. "Hello, I'm new to coffee, especially coffee that doesn't taste like coffee. Can I get something with all of the flavor, but half the fat? I'd really like one to boost my energy for a limited amount of time, have it taste great, be less filling, and not add an immeasurable amount of fat to my midsection if possible, please." This is a bit like going and ordering a fast food burger with cheese and a diet soda, of course, but it's what I do.

I don't know the difference between a cappuccino and a latté, and until recently, didn't know that chai was a tea and not coffee. All I need to know is, does it taste good, and will it be 100 calories or less? This may make for an exhausted coffee barista (a term I learned from a coffee commercial. Impressive, eh?), but I do eventually get what I want.

So for all those coffee connoisseurs out there, give me a break; I'm new here and a nicely typed cheat sheet for ordering skinny coffee drinks that don't taste like coffee would be handy. It would just make life easier on everyone in the line behind me. Until then, I will continue to go in and say, "I'll have a tall, skinny something that tastes nothing like coffee, but has coffee in it. You decide and surprise me. Thanks."

It seems there are many people who are in relationships that are complicated. This got me to thinking about my relationships. I too, am in a relationship that is complicated.

It's with... desserts. I know it's wrong. I know I don't need them, they are empty calories and only bring on extra pounds which is why my clothes don't fit. But... they call to me. It seems I can't go anywhere without seeing ice cream or strawberry shortcake. It seems wrong to not partake in something that is only good at one season a year.

I've heard that admitting you have a problem is the first step to recovery, which is what I'm hoping to accomplish. Maybe by admitting that this is a complicated relationship that needs to end, I can finally put away my desire to have desserts after every dinner. I remember a time in our relationship when dessert was a treat for special occasions. We didn't partake every day. It seems with the kids, they think it should be every day. I know, I know, I'm the adult here. What can I say? It's complicated.

Adventures in Cooking

When I was in high school, there was a movie called "Adventures in Babysitting" that I loved. I always wondered how it would be to have such adventures. Well, I'm getting a taste of one kind of adventure, as the family is now experiencing Adventures in Cooking.

Those of you who know me will know that my kitchen and I do not have a great relationship. There is a sign in my kitchen window that says, "My next house won't have a kitchen — only vending machines." I know how to make a handful of things well, and that's about it. One of those is lasagna and I make that once a year.

I'm not necessarily opposed to cooking per se; I'm more opposed to the cleaning up. Why mess up a perfectly clean kitchen when there are plenty of qualified people in restaurants who will prepare the meal better, AND clean up? That has always been my philosophy. When my girls were little and were messy eaters, we would eat out for the sole purpose of not having to clean up. Yes, I know that's rude, but I always tried to clean up a little before we left, and I'm a good tipper. I thought of it as my way of helping the economy.

I am no Betty Crocker. I do not see the benefits of a home-cooked meal if I'm the one cooking it. I see many benefits of eating out. A) I don't cook. B) I don't clean up. C) I help to boost the economy.

I like to try to get away with not cooking breakfast till 10 or 10:30. This way I can get away with making two meals instead of three, thus eliminating 20-30 minutes of my day in the kitchen, freeing up that time to either read books or otherwise plan to get out of more cooking.

Breakfast is the most important meal of the day. In this house, get it yourself, and while you are up, get me some too. Lunch is the next most important. So let's go out for some. Dinner... I suppose I could cook that, but do you really want me to? I'm just saying, vending machines or a drive-thru window outside of our kitchen window would be awesome. Think of the possibilities. Imagine opening your kitchen window and someone there to take your order and hand you your food. How cool would that be?

I love days when the kids all have things going on and there is no time to cook. I feel it's important for their well-being to be involved in extracurricular activities. I also feel it's important for our digestive systems that we eat out as often as possible. To that end, I'm getting involved in things to ensure another meal eaten out. I want to LIVE, man, I want to LIVE.

When I grow up and everyone comes to my house for Thanksgiving and Christmas celebrations, I hope they like Bob Evans, because the entire thing will be catered. Surely, ol' Bob started the entire franchise in his home; therefore, it's a stretch, but it's still considered homemade in my book.

But of course, cooking at home saves money. Dave Ramsey is our friend, in the loosest sense of the word, as we have never actually met him. The main thing I know about him is that A) His budgeting methods are helping us tremendously financially and B) He likes to wear blue shirts. My husband thinks he's a genius. Dave recommends e-meals, so we are now doing e-meals. If you do not know what this is, it's a website that will plan your dinners for you and give you a shopping list so you know what you will need to prepare each meal.

E-meals + trying to save money = I have been cooking... a lot.

Perhaps this is good financially, and also more healthy, but before you decide, let me list some of the meals that have been introduced to my children. Orange pancakes were last night's meal. This was good in theory, but not perhaps as orange-filled as one would think, as it called for orange zest. Do I own an orange zester? No, I do not. Do I even have a clue how to go about zesting an orange? No, I do not. I did, however, give it a good old college try, using what I had around. There was not any orange zest in the pancakes, but they were tasty and consumed nonetheless.

I thought I would start with the one that got rave reviews so you wouldn't think I was a total ninny. Now I will tell you about some of the meals that, although tasty to my sophisticated palate, were not some of my kids' top ten favorite meals.

Quick Italian Wedding Soup was the first one we tried. I thought it was tasty; the kids, not so much. They seem to have trouble getting past what things look like. If I were to blindfold them at mealtime, I'm convinced they would always eat what I prepare. As it was something new, and I was sure that no one would believe that I had created such a thing in my kitchen, I took a picture of it.

Later I had them try a Greek Chicken Casserole.

After begging with them to try the asparagus and refusing to let them leave the table until they took one bite, I decided to try one I was sure they would love. I will admit that I have never before cooked sweet potatoes and had to call a friend to ask her how to cook them. We ended up with pan-seared smoked sausage with steamed corn, baked sweet potatoes, and applesauce. The oldest was a little leery of the sweet potatoes, and I had to convince her that she does love them, that she merely forgot. This meal was her favorite.

All in all, it has been an interesting experience. We are all trying new things and stepping "outside our comfort zones," as they say in the world of food. After all, instead of eating a frozen pizza or spaghetti with Ragu tonight, the poor little darlings are going to be subjected to Old-Fashioned Pot Roast and veggies with dinner rolls. This should go a little better than the Spicy Sausage and Cauliflower soup from earlier in the week.

I think I have them properly brainwashed at this point, because the question is no longer, "What's for dinner?" or "Where do you want to go to eat?" More often I hear: "What new real food are we trying tonight?"

****

Statements and questions often said in reference to my cooking:

What kind of meat is this?

Is it supposed to look like that?

Are you sure we can't go out to eat?

Other people don't have to eat like this!

You know, I used to like spaghetti.

Why can't you cook like [insert another kid's mom's name] does?

You made cookies?! Who died?

Fitness Fool, or Foolishly Not Fit?

Exercise is Pain: Zumba Excuses

Today I have a few minutes to kill before I start running. OK, I am not really going to be running. I don't have the proper shoes on my feet for running. What I meant to say was, before I get in my car and drive around to all the places I need to go before I prepare dinner, I need to come up with five excuses why I can't get on the treadmill, and proceed to waste the rest of my evening.

I thought I would share with you the top 12 reasons why I won't Zumba. David Letterman does a top 10 list; I do a top 12. Maybe I'm more full of it than he is?

1. This is a true statement: I am on the Dave Ramsey plan and I don't have an envelope for Zumba. I do have a "blow money" envelope, but I like to use my blow money for very important things, like lunch money, if I run through my "food" envelope too quickly. I also use the blow money for things like sales on shoes.

2. I have been prohibited by NASA to dance in public.

3. I am a klutz and am quite afraid of turning the wrong way, causing a chain reaction of falling women.

4. I like to sing when a song comes on that I like. If I'm moving and singing at the same time, I could pass out from the exertion. I cannot afford the medical bills that could create (concussions can be costly and painful).

5. When I sing in the privacy of my house, the cats either hide or beg to be let out of the house. My singing could cause others to be psychologically damaged, and I cannot afford their therapy bills either.

6. I now know three people who teach Zumba. How do you choose without hurting someone's feelings?

7. Mostly because everyone else is doing it. I don't really like going with the crowd, unless it's chow time. I like to do my own thing. I'm a rebel like that.

8. I don't have the proper attire.

9. I tend to lose papers or forget them, so a "punch card" would not stay in my possession long.

10. I hate to drive, especially at night.

11. I don't know the appropriate amount of time between eating and exercising. Is it like swimming—do you wait 30 minutes?

12. I would... but I just don't want to.

I think I have several outstanding excuses NOT to do Zumba.

Zumba is what everyone is doing these days for exercise. If you don't know, Zumba is a class that you dance in. I have several friends who go to Zumba classes. I also have several friends who teach Zumba classes. All of them have tried to get me to take the class (which makes me wonder how I got so many friends that can dance so well). I have turned them all down. I have tried to explain it to them. They just don't seem to get it. Because the problem is that I lost all my "moves" in the post-natal drip.

That's right. I lost them all. When I was young, I took seven years of dance classes. I was not the best dancer in any of my classes, but I could move. At school dances, I was great. I may have had glasses as large as my face, and big hair to go with, but I could move on a dance floor. I loved going to all the school dances. It was a chance to hang out with my friends and do what I loved doing... dancing.

I still love to dance. I just don't do it well. In fact, my dancing has been reduced to a few token moves. I can "start the mower." I can "churn the butter." I can "Q-tip." I "hula hoop." I can't line dance at all. I can't do the mashed potato. I don't even mash actual potatoes in the kitchen, I buy them frozen. I can do many other things, but moving in a fashion that looks remotely like good dancing is not one of them.

Some skills that I do have are: I can talk on the phone, cook dinner, check homework, and let the cat out at the same time. I can do laundry, tell kids to do their chores, and catch up on my DVR recordings at the same time. I can cook dinner, read a book, and enjoy an iced tea at the same time.

Maybe this is the underlying cause as to why I'm not that good of a cook. I'm always doing other things while I'm cooking. I can play a game on the Wii, look up an answer on Google, and listen to a story by another child at the same time. I can chase a toddler while talking on the phone and fixing lunch at the same time. So my multitasking skills are up to par. But cooking and multitasking don't go together.

I dance around my house weekly. In my mind, I dance like a superstar. In reality, I dance like Elaine from "Seinfeld." It's a side effect from having children. I had kids and my feet got bigger, my rear got bigger; I lost my sense of smell and my ability to dance. I also became an even bigger klutz than I was before.

So when I dance, sometimes I run into the furniture. Also, I think stretching may be important. I would prefer to think I don't dance well because I don't stretch first, and not because I'm so old that I just can't move that way anymore (oh, who are we kidding?).

I am too scared to Zumba with people I know. I'll twirl when I'm supposed to turn, and smack right into someone, causing a chain reaction, and maybe breaking a body part of mine or someone else's. But I can't do it if I'm not on the phone, checking homework, and sweeping at the same time.

From Warrior 1 to Corpse Pose: My Day in Yoga

About eleven years ago, after child number two came along, it was time to try and shed some baby fat. I joined a gym and got somewhat fit by working the machines and taking kickboxing and yoga classes. Then life happened. I stopped going to the gym, because why go to the gym when you've lost the weight, right?

Another problem is that I'm a stress eater. I'm also an "I'm bored and that looks too good to pass by eater" — but that's beside the point. The fact remains that I did gain the weight back, and since college, have struggled with keeping weight off. My secret wish is that I had powers to move things with my mind, for the sole purpose of moving my tummy roll up to where my chest used to be.

One Christmas, my husband got tired of my complaining, so he decided the best gift would be a yoga mat and a big exercise ball. You can imagine my delight when opening up these gifts. Nothing else says, "Hey honey, you're getting a little chunky, why not fix that?" Needless to say, he never made that mistake again. The items in question have been in the back of a closet for the last 10 years.

My weight spiked up again six years ago, when I was eating for five. I wasn't even pregnant. I was caring for my mother, who was dying of cancer, as well as my husband and three kids, one of whom was just a year old. I ate my portion, the portion I made for my mom that she couldn't eat, and whatever was left on anyone else's plate. Then after everything was said and done, I spent a year losing 56 pounds. And swore I would never go back. I was making "the lifestyle change."

Three years after the great weight loss, I've gained approximately 20 of it back. I have not changed my poor eating habits, but I've started walking in the mornings again.

Then I was invited to go to a yoga class a friend was teaching.

I walked confidently into the new YMCA; yes, the one I have never been in. I could take the class for free, since they're always trying to drum up new members. I walked in and said that I'd like to take my friend's yoga class. The first question they asked was, "Have you signed a waiver?"

The first thought I had was, does one need a waiver for yoga? Isn't yoga supposed to be relaxing? I shrugged, signed my waiver, and walked in late for yoga class.

Here are my thoughts as I got into class:

"Hmmm… looks like we don't wear shoes for yoga, so my Skechers Shape-ups won't be toning my rear during this class."

"The class is looking pretty full already. Damn, they already saw me, I have to go in now."

"Uh oh, they are getting me a mat, so I'm in this thing for the duration."

"This may not be so bad, we have soothing music. We have my friend for an instructor, so she is less likely to make fun of me when I mess this up, fall over, and knock everyone else over."

"Boy, I hope that pizza last night doesn't come back to haunt me."

"Why isn't anyone else wearing a concert t-shirt?"

"I wonder what their success rate is of bringing people back, if my arteries are too clogged to do this, and my heart just stops?"

The class started, and I jumped right in. I'm not sure how often you have stood in a "warrior" position with your arms straight out at your sides, but let me just say, it really is harder than it sounds. Also, there is a lot to think about. Drawing your navel into your spine, breathing, keeping your shoulders down from your ears, and your knees over your ankles. It's completely exhausting!

Then at the end, you lay down and are expected to be able to relax completely. They don't tell you how to do this part. My mind was a whirlwind. I laid there placing bets with myself to figure out how long it would take me to get back up, IF that was even possible. The mere fact that I successfully finished the class without causing bodily harm to myself and others was quite a feat.

One year for Christmas, I got a Wii Fit (this time, it was something I asked for). The first time you get on the Wii Fit, it does an analysis of you. Strangely enough, it told me what I already know—that I had balance problems. It then asked me if I fell down a lot when I walked or if I run into things. My center of gravity is off. So what?

I am relatively accident prone. In college, I worked in a department store and often ran into the racks of clothing. I have fallen down stairs more times than I care to admit. THIS is the kind of girl I am.

All of this can only help with my fitness plan. Besides, I do have my own yoga mat now. It's purple, and perhaps I could get a cute outfit to wear to go with it. Plus, there is the promise of Starbucks afterward as a reward for not hurting anyone. I look forward to trying it again. I'll be the one concentrating on not breaking wind or falling over.

Muscles Don't Lie: "Kid, we've got some work to do"

When I was a child and I would move something to where it would hurt, I would tell my mom, "Hey, it hurts when I do this." She would then say, "Then don't do that."

I think of this as I look back and realize that I have now gone to three sessions of yoga. Yoga is pain. How bad can it be? I was completely unprepared for what I was getting myself into.

I apparently have muscles; in fact, entire muscle groups that I wasn't aware I had. These muscle groups of mine are tired. They have long relaxed with lack of use. Don't misjudge me here. I don't sit on my duff all day eating bon-bons and watching soaps. I am active. I walk in the mornings. I run my kids to all their activities. My television doesn't turn on until evening. In fact, on Facebook, all my farms, restaurants, and pets have probably died or closed due to lack of use at this point. I don't sit idle for long, is what I'm trying to say here. I can't be idle; it's not in my DNA. Even when I'm watching TV, I have to be doing other things at the same time.

Friends have told me that it's easy to progress with yoga. As you limber up, I suppose it gets easier. I have to tell you, I must be the least limber human on this planet. I go through the motions. The entire time, my body is screaming at me: "NOOOOO! Stop!" I don't, of course, because who wants to be the loser who drops out of yoga because turning yourself into a triangle feels like a form of torture? No one. So I stay.

I stay and try to remember to breathe. Sometimes I forget—with holding my shoulders back, pulling my navel to my spine, and all the other activating that is required—breathing takes a back seat. Fortunately, the instructor reminds us frequently to breathe, otherwise I may just turn blue.

Today we learned the half-moon. Not to be mistaken with a full moon (which is fun for teenagers in movies while driving down the road). The half-moon requires so much balance that I had to find a wall to prop my tired body up against, to avoid tipping over and thus causing a domino effect throughout the room.

So far, my favorite is child's pose. Even that can be a small torture in itself, as it pulls my shoulders to the point of breaking. This is what is known as a recovery pose. Recovery poses, I excel at. Not the corpse pose (or, lie down and play dead). That requires total relaxation. I'm wound tighter than a new yo-yo on Christmas morning. The moment I completely relax, I'm asleep. That's it, the only time. That's not to say that I don't or can't have a good time, I absolutely do. I just carry everything with me all the time.

Apparently, this is common in motherhood. As a mother of three, I am in a constant state of tension. Like a dog chasing its tail, there is always something that needs to be done, or someone who needs to go somewhere, or someone who needs to vent. Mom's taxicab runs all week long, the laundry is never caught up, my therapy sessions do double duty every other week, and I'm always running out of milk. It's impossible for me to get it all together. With all that milling around in my head, how on earth am I supposed to just lie on the floor and relax all my muscles, including the ones in my face? I know how to let go and let God, but He's got better things to do than my laundry, just so I can relax and read a book, or lie on a floor and play dead.

I do like this class, though. When my muscles stop begging me to quit the class, I do feel better. It's a good pain.

But I don't know if I will ever catch up with the yoga twins. You know the ones, right? They're the ones in your class who have all the attire; they can do all the moves like it's the most natural thing in the world. I know, I know, you're not supposed to look around, and you're supposed to go at your own pace. I've long since given up trying to catch up to anyone else. I think if I can be the best version of me, then I'm good with that.

Prize Fighter or "A" for Effort!

As I've already stated, I'm a bit of a klutz. What you may not know is that I can also be very determined, especially when it comes to beating a piece of machinery.

My first car was small and black and it went fast. It was a V8. We are talking horsepower here, people. Unfortunately, it was an old horse, and died about two months after I got it.

My next car was red. Beautiful, shiny, red, and sensible, and after college, it tried to kill me. I'm not kidding. The car was repelled by me. The car would start filling up with carbon monoxide, which, by the way, makes you feel dizzy.

Apparently it was the muffler. I have that effect on some machinery. (My stove tried to kill me in college also. Gas stove + hairspray = bad situation. I will never have a gas stove again.) This led to getting my first cell phone. The muffler shop gave away cell phones when you bought a muffler. That first cell phone was larger than my home phone is now. But I was very cool.

I don't remember what kind of car that first car was; not that it matters much now, but I have noticed that it's not just my cars that have grown over the years; I have too.

A few years back, I spent an entire year working on losing almost 60 pounds. I ate healthier and I exercised daily. I never felt better in my life. I told myself I would never go back. I would stay at it and keep fit.

The problem with feeling great is, once you are there, you think you will always feel that way. So, you tend to get too comfortable. "Surely, a bit of ice cream with fruit won't do much harm. Just a small piece of cake would be OK. I'll work it off." Then life happens. You get busy and you stop going to the gym. Fast food is easier, so you eat out more and more.

Then one day, you wake up and say, "WOW, these pants are tight! I must have left them in the dryer too long." Even when you dry your pants in damp dry mode, they're still tight. And then you have to face facts.

It was time for action. I started using the Wii Fit. This seemed harmless enough, until the bloody thing started groaning every time I stepped onto the balance board. Then you aren't as quick or strong or balanced as you thought you were, either, and that doggonned mii (my persona, or mii, as they call it) shakes its little head at you and pounds on the ground in frustration. I couldn't take it anymore. I did what any reasonable person would do, and tried the boxing selection. What better way to take out your frustrations?

Wrong! I couldn't get past two stars. TWO STARS? Really? I mean, I'm throwing punches here that would make Tyson himself proud. One time about ten years ago, I took a kick-boxing class to get fit. I know how to throw a punch. Well, I thought I did. I was punching my little heart out at the end, where you get to punch yourself into a frenzy. I threw my right. Then I threw my left. Then something went "SNAP!" Ouch, that's not good. So the left elbow snapped, and the bad shoulder slumped (an old college injury). As the days passed, the pain increased.

When I watched the movie "Ali" with Will Smith, I neglected to take note of the training involved, in being able to punch for all you're worth. I also forgot what happened to Wylie Coyote every time he tried to beat Bugs Bunny. Wii Fit Boxing 1, Heather 0.

Good news, though. The doctor says, and I quote, "I am NOT old, I am merely older than I was." I love that! It even made me forgive him for making me cry when he lifted my arm and I felt like it might be ripped off. So here I am, in my sling, taking medication that is supposed to have me pain-free and ready to start therapy in about 10 days. I can even type on the laptop with two hands, as long as I have the heating pad on.

So, maybe I won't be a prize fighter anytime too soon. But I think I get an atta-boy for giving it the old college try (I probably should have remembered what happened to the shoulder in college). I'm sure I'll remember these things, as soon as I remember to take the ginkgo vitamins for better memory.

Snow, Miis, and Ice Cream

The snow arrived this week. I will admit snow is pretty. If you ask anyone other than me to describe the snow, they will tell you that it was three to five inches. To me, that's a blizzard. The snow was coming down in huge flakes, and the roads were much too slick to drive on. The world as we know it should just take a few days off.

In this weather, businesses should shut down, so no one would have to go to work. The kids would stay home from school, and everyone one would have a much needed family day, courtesy of God. Those who enjoy playing in the cold white stuff would build snowmen and forts. Judging would take place and a prize could be awarded for the best effort.

Perhaps this is a fantasy built on watching too many children's shows, or perhaps it's the fact I just don't like driving in snow, and don't think anyone else should, either. Either way, it does sound nice, you have to admit.

I haven't seen any snowmen in the neighborhood yet. And you won't find them in my yard. My children and I are not much for the cold stuff. We just look outside and we get cold. I have had more coffee drinks, hot cocoas, and hot tea this year than I can ever remember having. All in my constant quest to warm up.

It goes without saying that I'd prefer to be making sand castles. Of course, there are days when even Orlando is in the sixties. I don't thaw out till it's at least 80. It's either my age creeping up on me, or maybe I just have a cold heart.

Or… it's not my fault at all. The high today was 26 degrees; with the wind chill, it was 0. And of course today's the day I had to sit in a cold car, in the school parking lot, until it was time to walk up to the school and retrieve my child for piano lessons. Fortunately for me, my friend teaches my child piano, so she had a steaming cup of cappuccino waiting for me, and a blanket in a chair by the fire so I could thaw out while my daughter had her lesson.

At the rate I'm going, one of two things is bound to happen. I will have to move into the restroom because of all the fluids, or I'm going to gain so much weight from all the cappuccinos and cocoas, I won't have to worry about keeping warm; I'll have hot flashes instead.

In my quest to fend off the repercussions that are sure to haunt me with all of these fatty drinks, I have started up on the Wii Fit again. Have I said the Wii Fit hates me?

I was informed when I started that it had been roughly 587 days since I had last used it, another reminder of my inability to stick with any method to stay in shape. It also informed me I was up thirteen pounds since I had last used it. Who wants to hear that? From a machine?!

I did watch "The Biggest Loser" on TV once, and those trainers are tough, but if you work hard, they give you props. My Wii Fit has a two-minute run. I will run my little heart out for two minutes, approach the heart attack zone, and because I don't swing the little controller enough, I can't get past one star. These are the ratings the system gives you for your performance. Obviously my performance is not very good, otherwise I would get past one star. My persona just drops her little head and pounds on the ground in frustration; it's not very encouraging. The only thing that keeps me going is that my jeans are still tight. I may have to resort to just heating up some water and drinking it with a sprinkle of Splenda to get warm.

In my twisted way of thinking, if I had a human trainer, I could visualize a target for my aggression. I could fantasize about hitting them while doing the boxing session. These miis are like cartoons. You can't fantasize about kicking in a cartoon's head; it doesn't work. It would be like kicking SpongeBob.

The snow, again, while pretty, is partly to blame here. It's cold and wet and makes the roads slick. While it's enjoyable to look at, through the window while sitting by the fire, I have no desire to go out and walk the three miles I should be walking, if it were warmer. I have a theory that you lose more weight if you exercise when it's warm, because you get hot faster, thereby making you sweat more. Maybe that's not how it works, but it is my excuse, nonetheless.

I also reason that ice cream with fruit should be a health food because you have your fruit group covered and ice cream is dairy. So what's the problem?

It Takes a Village … and a Lot of Time

The Neighbor Series

I live in a one-stoplight town. When we built our house, we were one of three on our street with no one beside us or across the street from us. When the other houses started going up, and their landscapes started taking form, it became apparent to me that "one of these things is not like the others," and I was the "one."

My thumbs have no green in them whatsoever. I buy plants, put them in the ground, and hope for the best. I realize that I am supposed to water them, but because they don't yell at me for food and drink like the children do, I often forget. I have an F.R.O.G. approach to landscaping: I Fully Rely on God to water them. If they need water, then it will rain.

I sometimes imagine conversations about what others must think of me and/or my yard. The following are some of those conversations, in letter form. While these conversations never happened anywhere other than in my imagination, they entertained me.

That said, I am blessed with wonderful neighbors, who I wouldn't trade for the world. I would be very sad if any of them really did move. And if I ever do move, I will be hard pressed to find neighbors that are as kind as mine.

1. Dear neighbors, I am glad you aren't home. I'm totally singing my heart out today while I clean my house. I am wearing my iPod so even I don't have to hear me sing. If someone were to come to the door, they would see a woman with wacky morning hair, dancing and singing into a spatula, pretending that towels are red carpet dresses, and shaking her rump, while cleaning toilets.

2. Oh neighbor, where art thou? I mowed the yard today. I enjoy listening to my iPod full blast while mowing the yard and then dancing around the yard. I also like to sing along. (I figure, I'm old. What are the neighbors going to say? That "Old lady Nestleroad has finally lost it"? News flash: I have three kids. I lost it a long time ago.) Yes, I did listen to the iPod while mowing, and yes, I did dance a little jig too, but I couldn't help it. I was all "waking up in Vegas," and "I want you to want me," and I couldn't control the need to dance and sing along.

3. Possible reasons why my neighbors want to move:

A. Our grass is half dead, but there are a few strands of green grass, and I refuse to mow them.

B. Perhaps they have witnessed my dancing while inside the confines of my privacy fence.

C. They have heard me singing. (I would think the dancing would be enough.)

D. They are tired of hearing me yell at the kids.

E. Lastly, those darn neighbors across the street have the same color siding.

4. Oh neighbor, where art thou? I'm sorry, my dear neighbor. It has been 5 days since I mowed, and you felt you needed to mow my yard on your side. I'm so sorry I can't mow my yard every other day.

I have children, you see. Granted, they are all in school now. However, if I do nothing to the inside of the house, it is likely it will be condemned. I do try to give the illusion that we do not live in squalor. Unfortunately, we kind of do. It's my family, you see. They don't understand the beauty of a garbage can or a kitchen sink. Also, they would wear rags if I didn't do laundry and go shopping for new clothes. I'm only trying to make sure they aren't ridiculed for their behavior outside of the home.

On another note, I behaved myself while I mowed. I didn't dance — not once. Nor did I sing along. So, you see, you don't need to move now. Think of all the hard work you've done to your landscaping.

I'm sure there are others out there like us. Our flowers may die and our yard may only get mowed once every week or 10 days. We need you to stay, to set an example as to how "grown-ups" take care of their yards. Personally, I feel if all the toys make it into the garage for the night, I've done my job improving the neighborhood.

5. Bad news for the neighbors (and one more reason you should be glad you don't live next door): I just discovered that in an empty room, with hardwood floors, there are great acoustics. Which means that… yes, I have been singing and dancing, and if I had drums, I would SO be a rock star right now.

6. Oh neighbor, where art thou? I realize I haven't mowed my yard for a couple of weeks.

However, if we could review, we did have a lot of rain, and it was cold. You haven't mowed in the last two weeks, yet you are out there mowing at 9:30 p.m. tonight. I'm thinking of letting my yard grow out like my hair. It looks so healthy right now, I want it to keep looking that way. I hope you don't mind.

7. Reasons you should buy the house next door: A. It's beautiful. The landscaping alone should be enough. B. The neighbor has a pool, so you should make friends with them. C. Said neighbor dances around the pool and thinks she's way cool because no one can see her. But she wouldn't notice if you watched anyway, so it's free entertainment.

8. Oh neighbor, where art thou? Our yard is mowed now, and we painted the swing set. We are cleaning up our act. It's been at least three days since I danced around the pool. I didn't even have the singing jam session in the house yesterday, in fear of offending you and forcing you to move out before you sell the house. Please don't move. The new people won't respect all of your immaculate landscaping. There cannot be more than one house like ours with more weeds than flowers. On the flip side, they are very nice weeds; they have flowers on them and are very hardy, so it's a shame to kill them.

I think the other neighbors will throw their hands up in protest if you don't stay and another family like mine moves in. THE HUMANITY of it all. Don't do it for me; think of the rest of them. Stay, we need you.

9. Oh neighbor, where art thou? Good news! I got the rest of my yard mowed today, right before the rain. I'm sorry you felt the need to mow my yard on your side last night at 9:30 P.M. I realized that you had in fact mowed my yard when I saw the grass on the driveway. I do apologize for not mowing quicker. Please forgive me and again, I'm sorry I'm not a better neighbor. P.S. I listened to the "Hannah Montana" movie soundtrack on my iPod the entire time, and I danced and I sang along, and I liked it.

10. Oh neighbor, where art thou? My husband was reminding me of our old neighbors from our first house. I wonder how that neighbor is. He was a great neighbor. Why, he brought his dog to my yard EVERY morning to fertilize my yard. Can you imagine the kindness and dedication that took? Every morning I could look out my sliding glass doors and watch him dutifully walking his dog over to my yard while I ate breakfast. It was quite a show. Some days we were blessed with it more than once. My, was he kind.

There was also that time we were having the septic tank cleaned out, before we moved. This same neighbor came over and yelled at the guy trying to get his truck up my driveway. You can imagine my surprise. I felt it was my duty to go enlighten him on my position on the matter.

I threw my clothes on (it was early in the morning and I had just a baby) and walked (stomped) over to his door. I informed him that while I appreciate the fact that the neighbors who lived there before us had moving trucks that had messed up his yard, that wasn't my problem, or my fault.

I also informed him that while my grass is greener over the septic tank—with the help of his dutiful dog—I would be happy to call the pound the next time he strolled into my yard. Fortunately, we moved not long after. Good news is... his wonderful companion did get to meet new friends. The people who bought my house? They had chickens. Isn't it nice how sometimes things just work out?

11. Excitement is in the air! No... wait... That's the smell of garbage, not excitement. However, excitement is in the neighborhood. The trash truck caught fire down by the neighbor's house and had to dump its load on the road. So, good folks, there is still time. They are reloading it as we speak, but if you hurry you may just make it for a last-minute drop. I called my neighbor. The conversation went like this:

<ring ring>

Stacy: Hello?

Me: Yeah, hi this is Heather. I was just calling because I just cleaned out the kitty litter and saw that your house was the new drop-off for trash. OK if I come down?

12. I secretly wish we could cement the entire front yard. I'm certain it would become all the rage.

The neighbors would all be doing it when they saw how nice it was to drive right up to the front door. Think of the possibilities. If our front yard were cement, we wouldn't have to worry about the neighbors thinking we were losers for not mowing more than a couple of times a month. I wouldn't have to mow the ditch out front. We could have flowers made from chalk drawings, and when it rained and washed them away, we could just draw some new ones. I'd never have to worry about my plants dying. And plenty of parking for company.

Oh sure, you naysayers comment that I'm crazy. The kids do need a yard. But they would still have the back and side yards. Plus, they would have the biggest playground for jump rope and hopscotch, and they could practice parking when they learn to drive. We would have the biggest basketball court in the neighborhood. Another perk—the neighbors behind us have huge trees, so they would never notice.

The rest of the neighbors would be so excited about my new parking (and the fact that they could borrow it on occasion), they would never complain to me about mowing: "Hey, it's April; you gonna mow, or are you waiting for the leaves to bloom on the trees first?" My response is that I'm sure there is another frost coming and the yard needs the extra grass to protect it till the weather is warm again. There is also the fact that I dumped the Christmas tree on top of the mower in December, and now cannot get to the mower, because the tree is too heavy.

Cement in the front, grass in the back. It's the new thing. A mullet for the yard! My genius is truly wasted on this perfect little town I live in.

I Gotta Go Back, Back, Back to Work Again...
But I Can Google With the Best of Them!

I re-entered the work force recently. I have been on a thirteen-year hiatus for the most part, with a few periods of work here and there. When my husband and I married, we agreed that: A) We would have children, and B) I would stay home to raise them until they were all in school. This is the year they will all be in school.

Now I'm scared! I tell my children that they need to plan for a career that does not involve saying, "Would you like fries with that?"

I have worked hard for thirteen years. I just haven't gotten paid for it. Today's society expects that you will work and not stay home. I feel fortunate that I was given the opportunity to stay home. However, I can't help but worry how potential interviews could go.

I rewatched the movie "Mad Money" with Diane Keaton recently, and it got me to thinking. If and when I would go on potential interviews, I'm sure I would be asked—depending upon the position of course—about my computer skills. I would have to be honest. I have helped type school reports for my children, I have my own blog, and I can Google with the best of them. I have no idea what Excel looks like; I don't know how to sell on eBay; I only know how to buy stuff, and if I knew how to decorate my blog differently, it would be WAY sassier.

Here are my actual skills: I can cook a meal from a box very well, I can sew to an extent, I have been a caregiver for my family and my mother, I clean my house, do the laundry, shopping, mowing, and decorating. I design jewelry, I run mom's taxicab, and I am pretty good at planning a funeral. Oh, and parties; I can plan a child's birthday party that will knock your socks off!

Now, what should I be when I grow up? This is the age-old question. Along with, "And where do you work?" You'll be in the mall, and you will run into someone you went to school with, or someone you just haven't seen in 10 or 20 years. What they always want to know is if they are better off than you are. "And where are you working?" is the first question out of their mouths.

I am standing there with three kids hanging off of me; man, this IS my work. All of the kids are staying with me, not running around, not eating the candy in the checkout lane; just hanging with me while I try to get away from the question before it is asked. Because of course, the person you're talking to has become a rocket scientist or a marine biologist, or maybe a cardiovascular surgeon.

I am happy for them. I am also happy for me because I got to stay home and get to know some of the greatest kids on the planet. I just wish people would say something like "That is great" or "It looks like you've done a good job!" instead of, "Oh, I see."

Semi-Middle Aged Woman Seeks Employment

Semi-middle-aged woman seeks a fulfilling career that she and her family can be proud of. Must fit into designated school hours and offer flexibility around her kids' school functions. Ideally, would entail a great deal of writing and very little math, and would be something that would require one to not wear men's clothing or high heels. This person is also afraid to drive in snow and has a bit of an affinity for gas station coffee drinks, as she can no longer afford the luxury of Starbucks and the peacefulness that four-dollar coffee provides.

Requirements for this dream job are:

1. Must have at least one associate degree (check). I have one degree in Medical Assisting and one in Marketing. This qualifies me to kiss boo-boos and have garage sales, which I have done successfully for the last fifteen years.

2. Experience working for an urgent care facility (check). Can handle many tasks at one time and also deal with snarkiness from adults.

3. Experience working at a department store, with an ability to pick out quality clothing, and also the ability to wait for a sale, so as not to pay full price (check).

4. Experience managing a husband, three children, two cats, two birds, a hamster, various fish, a newt, a puppy, and a dying mother (check).

5. Experience running a successful Taxi Service, for running to and fro to various events with children, rarely getting lost or losing track as to which function to attend on any given night (check).

6. Experience in keeping a home clean, aside from the never-ending laundry that accumulates each day (check).

7. A love of all things written, from fiction to nonfiction and poetry, especially when it rhymes, as these are easiest to remember (check).

8. Singing ability not needed, but gift of gab is key. Constantly grabs opportunities to share what her children are doing (and how much she hopes she hasn't messed them up for life) (check).

9. Must ask for time off if her kid is sick, because she is the one with the chicken soup.

10. Most importantly, she must love all people and will stand up for injustice. She will go to bat not only for the ones she loves, but will not be able to work in a place full of ridicule and demeaning people without speaking up.

****

My husband and I have started a quest. We are going through a "Total Money Makeover," Dave Ramsey's financial budgeting program. As part of this process, I want to contribute to the household finances. Unfortunately, there is very little that either fills my requirements or I qualify for. I'm reminded of the movie "Mad Money" where Diane Keaton finds herself in need of a job. Unfortunately, she also had been home for years, taking care of her family, and had a degree in art. The job placement people placed her as a custodian. She was appalled that, after all the years of taking care of her home and her family, that is what she was "qualified" to do.

Honey, I feel you. As mothers, we wear so many hats; it rarely occurs to us that when the time comes, in the real world, those hats aren't going to take us where we want to go. I once read somewhere that if you were to pay a homemaker what her job is worth, that she would make roughly $117,850 per year, according to Salary.com. And that is the median. Oh, if only we could make that kind of money!

There aren't that many jobs that are more challenging, scary, confusing, heartbreaking, exhausting, aging, and yet completely rewarding, as motherhood. But I find that when you've been with your children nonstop for 13 years, and they've spent the summer adding more gray hair and crow's feet, back to school is a time to look forward to.

My husband says I'm more valuable at home. I also believe this to be true. But I also believe that if we were able to get completely debt-free, we'd rather do it sooner than later. I am not going to make a difference if the only job I qualify for makes $65 a week.

I'm not sure how this will all play out in the end. It's going to be a long, hard journey, but one worth the making. So if you know of a job that a long-winded, high-strung woman could do to help to contribute to the family, do tell. I'd love to hear from you.

Party Time, or Hey! I Got a Job!

On a summer day in early August, I received a request from a friend and neighbor of mine. She had just taken a job as a preschool teacher and was in need of an assistant in her classroom. I won't lie and tell you that I jumped at the chance to help a friend in need. In all actuality, my first response to her was similar to "Oh? I'm so sorry for you. I'm sure they will find someone to work with you."

Was I already working somewhere? No. In fact, I had been home for two or three years after having worked in another preschool. Plus, I was kind of enjoying my life at home, even with my stressful schedule. For example, after the kids got on the bus, I would sit down to watch "Boy Meets World" and "What I Like About You." When the shows were over, I would get up and start my day. This would include lunch dates with friends, cleaning my house, and running my kids around. I had a good feeling that this would be the year that I would finally master the "churn the butter" dance while cleaning, and I would find the perfect hairbrush for singing into. So, as you can see, I had a lot going on.

On top of that, my year at the previous preschool was the single most stressful experience of my life. Becoming a mother for the first time was less stressful. Twenty-four hours of labor was less stressful. I was there during a time of transition, a time when you do not want to be an employee. It was not a good experience when returning to the workforce for the first time in many years.

That job actually caused me physical pain from the stress. I would wake up and not be able to move my neck to either side. I was determined to finish the year anyway. I did, but I had no desire to go back, to any job. I went back home where I was content. It was great. I was able to go on daytime dates with my husband. I could have quality time at home, redecorating and making it a place I could spend my time and not want to leave. And I didn't leave unless I had to.

It's funny, one minute you can think everything is just as you want it. Then God has another plan. I really like His plans. While having my conversation with my friend about this new job, I told her that I really couldn't do it because I had already committed to volunteering with MOPS (Moms of Preschoolers), so they would have to be willing to work around that schedule. She said, "Let me make a call and ask." Well, she made her call and I was told a little later that day that I should call the new director and talk to her.

Let me just say this new director happened to have the same name as the director at the previous preschool. So of course, I had questions about this woman. For example: Does she know that she has the same name as the woman who we dubbed "Satan's mistress?"

Suffice it to say, I couldn't have been more leery to call, but I did. After talking to her for a few minutes, I was surprised that she sounded excited. This was new. As we talked, I started feeling more at ease. She sounded hopeful and not at all like a crazy person. Maybe this could be good.

When she asked if I could come in to speak to her further, I said sure. I was there thirty-five minutes later. We chatted like old friends, and thirty minutes after that, I had the job. I threw every single excuse I could come up with to not take the job, and she responded with (good) reasons why I should take it.

So far, this experience has been what I had hoped my previous experience would have been. I love it. I look forward to it.

As I sit here writing this, I'm wondering what art project we get to do tomorrow. I kind of like having a reason to get dressed up again. I did spend a lot of time living in sweats, and while they are comfortable, they were getting old.

I think it's going to be a good year. A relaxing, let's go play in the paint, go on a bear hunt, have a snack, and read some stories kind of year. I wonder if maybe this is what was missing from the good time I was having before, alone, the opportunity to go and have a good time with others. God knew just what was missing. I'm so glad He knew the right time and right place to fill me back up.

Who Are You Working For?

When you are a stay-at-home mom like I was for many years, you are pretty much the boss of the house. Sure, I still was serving God, and consulting with my husband about things, but I was not working with the public at large. Like most people, I like things to go my way.

Recently, my husband gave me an attitude adjustment. I was getting upset about some things that were out of my control. While venting my frustrations about work, he said I needed to "leave work at work and decide at what point on the drive home to switch gears" to wife and mom. Then my husband asked me a question: "Who are you working for?" I looked at him funny, and then he said, "Do you work for God, the kids, or your teacher?" With a meaningful look, he told me that at that moment, I worked for myself.

And he's right. I have to say, once I figured out who I am *really* working for, I have been so much happier — not only at work, which I love, but also just in general. Because, you see, I do work for God. The way I figure it, if I do my job, no matter what it is, and it is pleasing in his eyes, I've accomplished something important. Ultimately, He is the one I seek to please. My life, while I have been given free will, doesn't belong to me. It belongs to Him. I am here at this time, on this planet, in this small town, because He designed it. He has a plan for me.

Doesn't that blow your mind? God has been working on me. I have been working with Him to change the tape that plays in my head. The conclusion is that I have listened to the lies for far too long. God sent His Son to die on a cross for our sins and that includes me; yes, even me. If I can get that through my thick skull, then I can also trust Him to lead me where He wants me to go. He will never leave me alone. I don't have to trust in myself. I only need to trust in Him.

I think everyone can use an attitude adjustment from time to time. We get caught up in the things of this world, the things that will all fall away once this life is over. We are blind to our own blindness.

So I ask you: "Who are YOU working for?" I ask not because I want to know. I want you to know. You need to know.
I want you to figure it out. I want you to decide WHO you are working for, so you can be happy, like I am. Once you stop living and working for yourself, and hand it all over, then you find the truth. Then you are working for the ONE who makes everything possible.

So… who are you working for?

Goin' For Broke

Dave Ramsey Believer: Chocolate Cake, Dave Ramsey, and Me

Wake me if I'm dreaming. Or perhaps I should stay asleep, for the dream is too good. I am feeling a bit light on my feet… even though I've been adding more weight for them to bear. (Note to self: German chocolate cake is good, but you don't need to eat half of it by yourself to fully appreciate its perfection.)

Perhaps contentedness cannot truly be put into words. For that is what I am, content. This Christmas was unlike all others in the past, because I am not holding my breath waiting for the aftermath to hit: the dreaded bills. "Don't get excited about that coming tax check, kid, you still have Christmas to pay for." This year, the other shoe is not waiting to drop. The shoes walked together, Christmas was officially over on Christmas. Because we paid cash for all of it.

It's an interesting feeling, really. In our society, we are taught that everyone has debt. It would be unnatural to not have credit card bills or car payments. Everyone has them; it's just a part of life. Perhaps it is for some, but for this next part of my life, we've decided to be unnatural. "Weird," if you will.

A couple of months ago, we were introduced to a book called *The Total Money Makeover* by Dave Ramsey. To tell you that reading it has changed our lives would be an understatement.

How do you describe the lift of a weight from your shoulders? How do you describe to your family and friends that all this time you've only been playing grown-up? That two college-educated individuals have only been pretending that they knew what they were doing?

When we were first starting out as a newly married couple, we were so excited about the future. What we found out eventually is that the future is now, and it's hard. It's also perhaps not as difficult as we had made it. My husband has a good job; we're blessed in that area. It pays well enough that I have been able to stay home and raise our children. They don't tell you this, but kids are expensive. They also don't tell you that bored housewives enjoy spending money. We were college-educated; we knew it all. Right? We, as well as everyone who knows us, have lived under the illusion that because my husband has a good job and we have a nice house, so we must have money. What I have tried to explain to some degree is that he would have a lot more money, had he not married me.

As a child, I learned a few things about money. Like groceries should only be bought with coupons, or if they are on sale. Never buy anything at retail price if you can't help it. But buying whatever you want, as long as it's on sale, is OK. Also, when buying things for yourself, it's important to hide them in your closet and eliminate all evidence so your husband doesn't get mad at you for spending money. That is how my mother lived her life.

I might add that for much of my childhood, she was the only one in her marriage working. New clothes and shoes were OK, food was secondary. Now, as a married woman who isn't married to a crazy person, I have no need to hide my purchases. Food is first and foremost, and clothing a close second. While I do love clothes and accessories, I love to eat even more. I especially love to eat out; the prettier the food, the better.

What I have learned from Dave Ramsey is that all those things are OK. But you have to pay cash for them. You have to tell your money where to go. Ours always told us where it was going and it would see us (or not) on the other side. My new buddy is Cash. It's still a new relationship and we are getting

to know each other. I still go out for a nice meal once in a while, but I pay cash. I go grocery shopping with cash. It hurts me to be separated from cash.

My best friend used to be my debit card. We still get along, but my old friends Visa and Discover and I have had a falling out. I got tired of having to work for their friendship. They always wanted something from me and never gave me anything in return. Who wants friends like that? If I want to go to lunch with a friend, I prefer that they truly want to go because they want to spend time with me. I don't want to have to earn the time with them by paying them off on time. As I get older, I am learning to enjoy my own company more, so I don't mind being alone. I don't need Visa and Discover to keep me company.

This Christmas, as I looked around at all God has blessed me with, my hot hubby, three beautiful kids, and a comfortable home, I realized that this is all I really need. Sure, I look forward to the day when I can walk on my lawn and know that I fully own it. Sure, I want to take a vacation to Disney that doesn't follow me home, but I'm OK waiting. The best things in life are worth waiting for, saving for, and enjoying guilt-free.

Yesterday, I went to the dentist. A girl that works there asked me if I was working anywhere. I said that I was staying at home because I don't work well and play well with others. At least not on a regular basis. That is my joke—sort of my reason for staying home. Do I think I would enjoy working in a place where everyone got along and enjoyed their job? Absolutely.

But it's not reality. I prefer to work alone, that way the only person I can upset is myself. I think I'm doing all right. The kids are fed and they are fine. My house is clean for the most part, and at least once a week, my cats are entertained with music and dancing by yours truly.

Maybe I don't have a monetary income. But as Dave would say, I am a gazelle, and I am intense. My husband and I are a team. We are working together to change our family tree. He goes out and works, I am learning to cook at home more and we both find ways to save money on the things we need. I am also getting fond of my new friend, Cash. She has a lot to offer, and she never fails me, as long as I treat her with respect.

On the Way to Financial Peace, There Are a Lot of Blue Shirts

In my quest to become a "grown up," my husband and I have been having a "Total Money Makeover," courtesy of Dave Ramsey. I have read one of his books, the *Total Money Makeover,* and am currently reading another, *Financial Peace.* We're also attending his Financial Peace University workshop at a local church.

What I am learning is that even though my husband and I are both college graduates, we aren't really very intelligent when it comes to our finances. This is improving now, and it's exciting to see the difference it has made in both our finances and our relationship. We sit down and do our budget together. We discuss and plan and get excited by the changes we are observing. What's even better is that our family thinks we are crazy… so, according to Dave Ramsey, we are right on target.

The only downfall I can see from this is that we do not have many conversations currently that do not involve Dave in some way. "What would Dave say?" is a common phrase during financial discussions.

I am a little concerned that while we have a clothing fund, the clothing fund will start being used to purchase only blue shirts, like Dave's wardrobe. In every video we have seen of Dave in our Financial Peace University class, he wears a blue shirt.

While my husband isn't a shopper, I'm a little worried that I'm going to wake up one day and all he will own are blue shirts, like Dave Ramsey. Seriously, what is with all the blue shirts? Sure, they match his eye color. But I have to wonder exactly how many blue shirts are there? Are there seven of them on a rotation? Does he own only the one blue shirt? Is that one of the ways he got so financially fit? Does his wife have to wash the one blue shirt every night before an event? These are questions I ask myself.

We aren't getting out much, so that's sort of a bummer. Dave says we have to live like no one else, so later we can live like no one else. I'm ready to get to the other side. Currently, I'm going through my things to see what I can sell. Dave says I need to "sell so much that the kids think they are next."
I recently broke the news to my 14-year-old that she needed to start saving money now so she can pay for half of the car she wants when she turns 16.

You can imagine the reaction I got: "Mom … I'm fourteen!"

I replied with, "And isn't it about time you got a job?" I had a job from the time I was eleven years old and I worked all through high school and college. If I had been given the opportunity to continue on my rampage, I probably would have followed that with, "And I walked up hill both ways to get to those jobs, too."

Everything I have read by Dave so far has made sense. Not only that it works. The Bible says in Proverbs 22:7: "The rich rules over the poor, and the borrower is servant to the lender."

We finally decided we would rather not have everything we brought in just going right back out to our lenders. It's just too stressful to live that way. I owe a thank you to Dave. I do like him… and his blue shirt. No matter how many of them there are.

Random Observations

Sleeping

You know when the person you love is asleep, and they look so peaceful? You look at them and think, "What a miracle they are in my life, they are so beautiful!" When I look at my children and my husband, I think those things.

Unfortunately, that's not how I look when I sleep. Those who have had the misfortune to see me asleep can attest to what I'm about to tell you. Once, in high school, I fell asleep on a friend's couch. She came in and had an entire conversation with me, until she realized I was asleep. I sleep with my eyes half open, and my hair looks like my finger poked a light socket. My arms go over my head like a frog and I tend to take over the bed, blankets, and pillows. Don't forget the, uh, sound effects.

I often wonder what my husband sees when he looks at me while I'm asleep. Years of marriage have blinded the poor guy. I believe this because he willingly wakes up to me every morning and does so day in and day out.

That's what love does to us, I suppose. I can have the worst day with my children and be so furious with them, but once they fall asleep, and I look in on them before I turn in, I think to myself, "How am I worthy of this?" They are such a huge part of my life. Why God felt I deserved them, I will never know.

It's the same with my husband. Neither of us are "spring chickens" anymore, as he likes to say, but when I look at him, I see that young handsome guy that has always made my heart go aflutter and my knees go weak. The few flecks of gray in his hair and the snoring at night are small tradeoffs in comparison to the man God has given to me to share a life with.

Of course, the ups and downs (and the fun of it all) make up the journey. God has led you to go on. It's not all fireworks and sparklers; it's what you do when the sparklers burn out and it's just the two of you — holding hands and picking up the messes that are made along the way.

Have Pants, Will Wear Correctly

My family and I just got back from a getaway. My husband and I take our children to an amusement park every year. This year, we went to Kings Island and took in a Cincinnati Reds game. A great time was had by all, but on this outing I discovered something disturbing.

While walking through said amusement park, which also has a water park, many people were walking around in swim attire. Usually, this means shorts and a shirt for the girls, and shirts with swim trunks for the boys. This year, however, I noticed something else.

We have all seen those kids with their pants hanging down. That "American Idol" contestant once wrote a song about it. What I did not anticipate was to see this trend on girls. The shorts are getting so short that if you are over the age of 18, you can barely find a girl wearing a pair of shorts that don't look like they belong on a six-year-old. I saw more than one girl walking around the park in a bikini top and short shorts that *they didn't even bother to zip or button*. Honestly? The shorts barely covered their bottoms, and if you are just going to leave them open in front, why bother? Are the shorts too tight? Were they embarrassed to lie on the ground to get them zipped? Were they just too lazy to button them? Are their opposable thumbs not working, and they were afraid to ask for help? Have we all entered the Garden of Eden and decided to walk around naked? Surely, someone has answers to these questions.

When I get ready to leave my house, I think about what I'm wearing. I have seen enough episodes of "What Not to Wear" that I can sometimes hear Stacy and Clinton in my head assessing what I've chosen. I always determine if what I've chosen is appropriate for the occasion.

I don't go around town looking like I'm going to the gym, if the gym isn't my destination. I don't wear short shorts, first of all, because I'm not six years old, and secondly, who wants to see an old lady with a half-moon coming out of her shorts? I don't wear softball clothes to church. I wouldn't dream of going to a doctor's office without makeup and nice clothes, because even if you are sick, you aren't dead, so don't look like it. You get the picture. I try to be both age- and location-appropriate. And though I have a wig with long hair that I adore, I never wear it in public. Sometimes I wear it around the house with my tiara so I can feel like a princess. But you didn't hear that part from me.

In "Steel Magnolias," (one of the best movies ever made), one of the gals says she hasn't left the house without Lycra on her thighs since she was a teenager. Another woman responds that is because she was raised right! Which leads me to wondering… who has raised these girls to think it is OK to walk around with their shorts open? Honestly, doesn't anyone parent their children anymore? You can make the argument that these girls were probably college-age, as they were with boys, and without parents, at the amusement park. What about their upbringing? Didn't their father or mother ever once say, "There is no way you are leaving this house looking like that!" As a mother, I had an overwhelming desire to grab large towels and cover them up, call their mamas, and tell those boys to close their eyes. What happened to dignity and self-respect?

OK, it's obvious now that I'm old. And I am old-fashioned. I have daughters, who, if they ever once thought about leaving the house or walking around in public dressed like these girls, they know I would tie them up so they would never leave the house again.

No boy who wants to date my daughter would want to date a girl who walks around with her body on display for the entire world to see. Of course, any boy who even wants to consider taking one of my daughters on a date will have to pass inspection. If they bring them home late, there had better have been both a phone call and a tow truck involved. If they come in even looking at my child inappropriately, they will be told to turn right around and leave. This old bird is having none of that! I do know how to swing a frying pan, and I'm not afraid to use it.

So please listen to me, young gals (or even older gals who dress much younger), think, would you? When you're dressing, ask yourself, do these pants fasten? Do they cover all the vital parts? Do I want to walk around with my shirt so tight and low-cut that one wrong move results in a wardrobe malfunction?

I understand being away from home and not thinking you will see anyone you know. But do you really want people you don't know looking at what God gave you? Even thinking about going to the OB/GYN makes me nauseous. So I cannot imagine the train of thought that goes into dressing so scantily. I don't even wear anything less than a one-piece swimsuit in my backyard, behind my privacy fence, if we have company. In fact, I don't get in the pool, and wear a cover-up the entire time, if we're in mixed company. If I do get in, when we have anyone over, usually it's because I get pushed in, or it's so hot I can't take it. But I cover up immediately after getting out. I'm pushing 40 here; whatever I have left isn't anything anyone wants to see anyway.

Think, girls. We have clothes for a reason—use them wisely!

Musings

1. You ever wonder about people who get mad at servers at Chinese restaurants because they don't speak English very well? Uh, hello, aren't you kind of on their turf?

2. Do you ever wonder about people who wear shirts that say "I'm with stupid," but they are walking alone?

3. Things I wish I could still do:

Speak French
Shorthand (it was so much fun)
Sit ups.

4. Things that are a bummer when you get old:

Knees creaking when you go up or down stairs.
You can no longer remember what you forgot.
Five pounds may as well be 50, because it's not going anywhere.

5. While looking through old pictures, I made several discoveries about myself:

My hair has changed in both length and color several times over the years.
I have been every weight under the sun.
Me + dance costume = extremely embarrassing photos, but not as embarrassing as the Madonna phase my cousin loves to remember fondly. (We won't discuss the Michael Jackson era, either.)

I always look better in pictures where I'm outside. I believe it's because there are other things around to look at to distract from the squinting of my eyes.

Also, I believe that I always look happiest when surrounded by my family, who hates picture day, but goes through with it because it's my favorite time of the year.

6. I once saw a commercial for a website called mylife.com. Apparently, you can go there and see who is looking for you. If someone is looking for you, do you really want to know? It sounds kind of like a double-edged sword to me. Also, why wouldn't they just look in the phone book? And if you aren't listed, can't they just take the hint you don't want to be found? One of the amusing things about the commercial is that the lady in the commercial is excited that there are 7 people looking for her. Ever wonder, lady, if they are bill collectors? She says, "It may be an old boyfriend." If it is, does she not remember what made him an old boyfriend in the first place? I would just like to say that I don't want to be found. Of course, I'm not big into reunions, either. If I want to talk to you, I'll call, email, or text. I may even send snail mail.

Keepin' the Faith, But Not Like Billy Joel

God Had a Better Plan

I grew up an only child, in a home that was far from happy. My mother tried to make a family with these ingredients: One woman, one man who hates kids, one stubborn and smart-mouthed kid. Mix, stir, and shake, till chaos ensues.

I spent my entire childhood fighting. Fighting with mom, fighting with her mentally unstable husband, and fighting to get through school alive. I dreamed of having an older brother to beat people up for me (because I was far from the popular kid in school) and a little sister, so I could do her hair.

When I was a teenager, I knew three things for certain;
1) I would never get married, 2) I would never have kids, and
3) I would move as far away as possible. If you went to school with me, you would often hear me say things like "You know, statistics say if your parents don't have kids, you won't either." I was going to go college, become a buyer for Bloomingdale's, live in the city, and eat food I couldn't pronounce. I would spend my free time shopping, and my work time shopping—for the world.

Sometimes I think about what would have been, had my life gone down that path. As a now- married woman with three kids, who didn't move but 10 miles from the house she grew up in, I would have had an exciting life, comparatively.
I certainly would have had the best wardrobe money could buy… and, I would have died alone. I need only to look at my children's faces and hold the hand of my husband to know that God had a better plan for me.

I would have missed out on so much had I followed the path I said I wanted for myself. Granted, this one's not all been a path of roses and chocolate. My oldest child was an emergency C-section, and my middle child didn't speak for four years. After all that, I was sure I was done. I sold every baby item we had, and said, "I have all I can handle." God had a better plan for that, too. Five years after my youngest daughter was born, we had a bouncing baby boy. I shudder to think what my life would have been without any of them. I cannot imagine a life where they don't exist.

I have lost my grandmother, my mother, and two of my aunts now, and the only grandfather I ever knew. Like in my childhood, I see my biological father on birthdays, Christmas, and special occasions. I have no brothers or sisters, except three stepsiblings I rarely see, and didn't get till I was 25.

Would they drop everything and come if I were in need? I'm not sure.

I have read "Friends are the family that you choose for yourself." I believe that is true, but I also believe that God has a hand in sending them your way. In that respect, my family is overflowing. I have a sister; I picked her out myself. She lives an hour and a half away, and we talk weekly. She will drop everything and come if I need her. I would do the same for her.

I didn't become the buyer for Bloomingdale's; I became the buyer for the family instead. I didn't get a degree, but I can kiss boo-boos and have garage sales with the best of them. I didn't move to the big city, but now I'm scared to drive on interstates, so that worked out well, too.

Although my beginnings were far from ideal, God had a better plan. All those things helped to form who I have become today; a happily married woman with a real family, just like I always dreamed about, but never thought possible.

Groundhog Day: What Is This, Miami Beach?

My husband and I LOVE the movie "Groundhog Day" with Bill Murray. If it is on TV, we watch it, and always on Groundhog Day.

What I love about this movie is the way it covers so many emotions, and what would you do if you had to live one day over and over again. His character, Phil, gets stuck covering Groundhog Day as a weatherman, over and over again, until he gets it right. He goes through every thought process, between what can he get away with and survive, to killing himself to make it end, to figuring out that maybe this life isn't just about him. Until the moment when he figures out that he needs to look outside of himself to those around him. Then he can move on to February 3.

This makes me contemplate all the days of my life. With all the peaks and valleys, what one day would I want to relive over and over again? What one day would I rather not, and what would I do differently. How would I handle that?

Of course, I think of the days that each of my children were born. Perhaps that first time around, I wouldn't have waited till it was too late to say "OK, I've had enough, I'll take that epidural now." I think about my wedding day, and maybe I would have just acknowledged before then that me and heels are not a good combination, and probably would have just had the dress hemmed to fit with the Keds I ended up wearing down the aisle (as it was, I had to kick the dress while walking to keep from tripping on it). I think about all the hurtful things I've said to others, and wish I could reel those back in. I think of the mistakes I've made, and the challenges I've walked away from instead of walking forward full throttle.

I think of every mistake, every wrong word, every wrong turn, and then I stop. What good does it do to look back? What good does it do to think of the things that I should have done differently, that can never be changed? I think the moral of the story here is not how we could change the mistakes we've made, but how we can look at those mistakes and keep from making them again. How, by looking forward, and not looking back, we can improve and become better people. I can no sooner go back and change the mistakes of my past than I can change the order to the stars in the sky.

I have asked for forgiveness. My heavenly father has forgiven me, and for that matter, knew I'd make mistakes anyway. He was still willing to send His Only Son to die on the cross for me. What good does it do to think and dwell on things that God has already forgotten? I can only learn and move forward, praying all the way that as long as I stay on the straight and narrow path, I can try the best I can to keep from straying from the path He has set for me.

So again this year, I will watch "Groundhog Day." I will laugh, and I will think. But not about what day I would live over and over again. I'll think of the days I will (hopefully) be given to do the best I can with. After all, isn't that why we look forward to Groundhog Day? New beginnings? The end of winter and the beginning of spring? It can be cold out there. How will you warm it up?

To Be a Tree, Or to Be Me

I think if I could be anything, I would be a tree. Always reaching for the sky, looking towards heaven all day, swaying in the breeze. A tree doesn't mind the weather, doesn't mind if you climb to make your way to the top. A tree provides shade from the sun, and a home for those who need it. Yes, I think being a tree would be nice, because even when it's cut down, it knows it still serves a purpose.

As I look out my window today, the trees still have a good supply of green leaves. When walking along the walkway now, I notice more and more leaves falling from their branches and turning brown and crunchy under my feet. Fall isn't far off, and soon all the leaves will be red, yellow, orange, and brown.

I like fall. In some ways, it's a shedding of old skin. Spring is rebirth, summer a time to flourish, but as I think about the impending winter, I never look forward to it. Trees, just like people, go through changes. Some of them may not be to our liking, but necessary nonetheless.

Seasons change, people change, moods change. I once heard someone say that "she changes moods faster than she can change her underwear." It must have been a teenage girl they were talking about. Or perhaps they were talking about women in general. I know my own moods can change with the weather. When it's sunny, I'm happy. When it rains, I feel down. When it snows, I feel confined.

And so it goes every season. The trees lose their leaves, and I think how sad I am about it and how I wish it were spring. But I know the rebirth will come.

I tend to have a better outlook when I have a Bible study to go to. I do better when I'm told what to do, and if there are others to hold me accountable. I'm the kind of person who will do what you ask, but I need direction. While I tend to talk to God during the day, I don't spend time reading in the Word, unless I have direction and know what to read. It also helps to have a leader to explain and make sure I understand what I've read. While I can read a book all day long and retain the information, when reading the Bible, I have a hard time with the fact that God wants me. (I can't imagine why. I've had a messy life.) I don't believe I deserve it. I'm a sinner. I mess up all the time. But I know of rebirth. I know I've been washed clean.

Now, people don't necessarily get "reborn" every spring like trees, but wouldn't it be nice if they did? In church, we learn we are reborn through Christ Jesus our savior. We are saved, baptized, and reborn through our faith in him. Every time I see someone get baptized, I cry. To me, it's like watching a birth, only without the mess. But it's sometimes the messy parts that lead us to where we ultimately need to go. Life is messy, and sometimes it takes a good cleansing to get it right.

I think we should re-up, like the trees in the spring. I think it could make a real impact on our lives, especially on the lives of non-believers. Everyone gathers together at the river, we fall to our knees and ask for forgiveness, and then get baptized again. Continue in your studies all year, and ask for forgiveness when you need it. Praise him all day, every day, but once a year, come together as a group and reaffirm your commitment as a body of Christ.

Put that on the news. Show the leaders of the world that we, as a body of Christ, are coming together, and this is One Nation Under God. The founding fathers of our country wanted religious freedom. We received it, then we chucked it out the window by allowing the non-believers to say that they didn't want "In God We Trust" or any other religious statements in public areas. Well, too bad. I'm insulted by the non-believers thinking they can take my religious freedom. This is where the standing firm needs to happen; someone to say no. They are bullies, the way I see it.

There are so many who seem to have it all together. I am not one of those people. I have very little together. I also know that most of the time others seem like they're all together, but it's an illusion. People tend to portray what they want you to see. Sometimes you miss the fact that the base has rotted out, because all you can see are the pretty green leaves. There are no perfectly formed trees, so finding perfect people is pretty futile. They don't exist. There has been only ONE perfect person on all the Earth, and he died so that we can find our way to the Father once again.

So why do we keep striving to be like those who seem to have it figured out? Why do we try to conform to what we aren't chosen to be? I suppose I could spend my whole life wondering what my purpose is. In "The Five People You Meet in Heaven," Eddie says he was "just a maintenance man."

He never went anywhere. He didn't do a lot with his life. But then he goes and meets five people and begins to understand about his life.

My husband is just now reading the book, and we talked about who we thought we'd meet when we get to heaven. I'm not sure who would be waiting to enlighten me about everything. I know who I would like to see, but mostly, I think when I get to heaven, and I get to look into the face of God, it won't matter so much who explains anything. I think that when I get to be with my Father, it will be like coming home.

Perhaps longing to be like the trees that look towards heaven is what we should be doing, instead of looking to see who's beside us, while we're looking up. The way I figure it, God wants me to be happy. The people I love make me happy, so they will be with me again someday. Surely, the God who can move mountains, turn water to wine, part the Red Sea, and bring my mother (who never went to a church my entire childhood) to soften her heart so she could go home to be with Him, the rest of my family should be a breeze.

God places people in our lives for a reason. We are here to learn. I guess what I've learned so far is to not question. I just believe that HE is the one in charge, and I don't worry anymore.

What if You ARE Someone?

In Sunday school one day, we were discussing people's perceptions of us. I have often wondered what people see when they see me. Do they see what I see? Do they see what God sees? Do they see something completely different? I wonder if they see the truth, or what they want to see.

Every morning I look in the mirror and I see aging. I see my mother, if truth be told. Often, I look in the mirror, and say "Hi mom." It's funny, isn't it? The passage of time. It slips away in this busy life and we hardly notice. Until one day we look in the mirror and see our mothers (or our fathers, as the case may be).

Mostly, it's the eyebrows. They are a problem. When I was young, I couldn't wait to be old enough to get them taken care of. Then, they were like little furry caterpillars that had taken up residence on my face.

Now I'm old. They don't grow. In fact, they may be thinning. Other than the stray here and there, I fear I may have to draw them on soon. Can you imagine? I could be like all those women that take their eyebrows completely off and draw them back in, on purpose. That should be a good look for me. Imagine the irrational, admittedly ugly duckling with low self-esteem, with a tendency to overreact and use sarcasm as a way of avoiding confrontation, now with no eyebrows. That should boost the morale, don't you think?

Although, it should take the focus off the fact that my spare tire is back. I shouldn't have to worry about drowning, as I have a built-in flotation device around my waist. Yep, I'm feeling better about myself already.

When I look in the mirror, I see someone who really just doesn't have it all together. I wait too long to color my hair. I fall off the wagon every time when it comes to diets or "lifestyle changes." I see a scared little girl who wants to stand out just enough for people to be her friend, but not so much to draw attention. I see a mother who would do anything at all for her kids, and struggles with letting go. I see someone who starts things that rarely get finished.

But in light of all of that, I wonder what would happen, how different my life would be, if I looked in the mirror and saw what God sees. And taking it further, what if the people around me could do the same? What if when we all looked at each other, we saw each other as God sees us? As beautiful. As wonderful, unique creations designed by God. As someone worth dying for.

Did you know? Did you know that you are loved so much that you are worth dying for? Have you ever thought of yourself that way? That would be a no, for me. It escapes me how God could still love me. But of course, I am human and I don't think like God. Which is a relief; he's much more forgiving.

I wonder if we could all look at ourselves and those around us, not as our human eyes see the outward appearance, but maybe what we have the potential of being. How God sees us. As His beautiful creation, someone worth dying for, someone with potential to fulfill His will for our lives.

How amazing could our attitudes be towards others, as well as ourselves? Could we all see each other as works in progress? As people worth getting to know, and love, regardless of social status? What if... we were just loved creations of God? What if?

Juggling

This week, I have some time on my hands. This week I can afford to be sick, or accidentally injure myself while trying to prepare a meal, check homework, and listen to a recount on the day's events at school.

Last week, I did not have time for these things. Last week is when I had the list of things I had volunteered for, all the things I didn't volunteer for but said I'd do anyway, and the unexpected things, all come to a head.

You know that expression, "don't drop the ball"? I think of all the things on my to-do list as balls. Up goes one ball (Bible study: need to get my quiet time in and my homework done); up goes another ball (family ball: need to take care of the hubby and kids); up goes another ball (household ball: need to get my chores done and the meals prepared); up goes another ball (extended family and friends ball: need to make the calls and uplift in any way I can). Volunteer ball: two groups of MOPS meetings; need to take care of those kiddos. Volunteer ball again: working the school book fair two days.

The balls just keep coming, and you balance. Last week, I felt a bit like the Cat in the Hat, with more balls to juggle, because they were being thrown at me from every direction. But this week was exceptional. We lost a loved one in the family, and a friend lost a beloved mother as well. So up goes another ball, a funeral, be strong and hold yourself together ball, while working in the visitations and funerals.

Add in the accident that took me to the ER, and the consequent doctor's appointment, and the sore throat and cold that set in, and I was starting to lose my balance. Of course, I didn't slow down or stop moving like I was told to do, so I could get better more quickly. (As a child, I was stubborn, and obviously haven't grown out of it.) My husband never slows down when he is sick. He says it's mind over matter; if you don't accept it, you won't be sick, and you can just keep going. So I kept going. But by Saturday, I was a mess.

I was a vision. One bandaged finger, I sounded like there was a cheese grater in my throat, and when I woke up Saturday, one eye was swollen shut. Ah, so when they said I should rest, and let myself heal, that's what they meant.

You know those people who need to be hit over the head until they get it? That would be me, especially when it comes to me. Because of course I can do it all, and I can do it all myself, I don't need any help.

So in my quiet time, I kept hearing the word *juggling* being whispered to me this week. How often do we just keep juggling, without asking for help, or even asking for strength to do the things we think we need to be doing? I don't like to disappoint people. So I juggle. So I hear God whispering, *"You're juggling, Heather."* But I still didn't ask for help, because I was sure I had it covered.

But had I listened to God, and had I listened to the doctor, how much better I'd have felt. We get so busy these days that sometimes even with our eyes wide open, we can only see the "stuff" we have to do, or the "stuff" that is getting in our way. We don't stop; we keep pushing and going forward.

Psalm 46:10 says, "Be still, and know that I am God." Maybe sometimes only with our eyes closed, can we be still long enough to know that He is God, and even if we think we may have things in control, we don't… but that's OK. He's got this.

So, lesson for the week: Stop juggling unless you're in a clown suit and wearing a red nose. There is no need to juggle, especially if you are unprepared and unqualified. He's waiting for you to ask for help. Do it.

Dear Lord,

Thank you for the lessons you teach me. Help me to never get so busy that I don't take time to stop and ask You for help when I need it. Thank you for closing my eyes so I could be still long enough to know that You are God and You have everything under control.

In Your Holy name, I pray.

Amen.

Getting on the Boat

One of the movies I like to watch lately is "The Proposal," with Sandra Bullock and Ryan Reynolds. In the movie, they go to Alaska to see his parents, and they need to take a boat to get to their house.

The scene goes a bit like this:

Margaret: "I'm not getting on that boat."

Andrew: "That's fine. I'll see you in a couple days."

Margaret: "You know I can't swim."

Andrew: "Hence, the boat!"

This cracks me up every time, and then it gets me to thinking. She is afraid of getting on the boat because she can't swim. He can't understand why, because she won't be swimming, she'll be on the boat. How often do we "miss the boat," or flatly refuse to get on the boat, because of fear?

I have been having several "duh" moments lately. Moments where I feel like God is just pointing things out to me and I feel like, "Oooh, I get it now. That's what I'm supposed to get from this." For me, it helps if I can talk it out.

I was doing my Bible study last week and I was having some trouble understanding what I was supposed to get from it. So I called a friend and asked her about it. As we spoke, the light bulb went off. (There may have been a heavenly choir that began to sing in celebration.)

My goodness, how many boats have left the dock without me on them? How many boats have I watched leave the dock while I waved and said, "I'm not ready, I can't do it. I'm not good enough." I think I've missed every boat that came to the dock… or maybe I never even went to the dock. Fear has been so prevalent throughout my life, and I think I'm starting to understand why.

When you are a child, we learn what we live. If you are told something long enough, you eventually take it as a fact. I try every single day to tell each of my children how special and wonderful they are. I tell them they are beautiful and smart and kind, and such a gift to my life. Because those are the things I want them to believe about themselves.

Those are not the things I grew up hearing. My mother married a man, not my father, who told me daily that I was ugly, I would never amount to anything, and no one would ever want to marry me. Well, I have been happily married to my hottie hubby for almost sixteen years. I take no credit for that—it's a total God thing. When I look in the mirror, I see flaws. When I think of doing something, I usually give up, because I'm certain I will fail—mostly because that's what I was told would happen.

Here's what I'm figuring out. I married an incredible man. God brought just the right man to be my partner in this life. And this wonderful man must see something beautiful and worthy in me, or he wouldn't have married me. I usually fail at things, only because I quit or give up before I have any chance to fail or succeed, because I am equally afraid of both scenarios. I suppose I'm more afraid of succeeding than I am of failure. If I try something and fail, it's really not going to change my life. And I'm pretty comfortable with my life as it is. If I were to attempt something and succeed, it could greatly change my life, so I've never known if something new was worth the risk. I am an optimist, which is the weird part of my lack of self-esteem. What if all of my dreams could come true? What if I got pulled from my comfort zone?

I am a walking contradiction. I don't want to try something because I will probably fall on my face. I don't want to try something because of the off chance I succeed. There you have it. I have let the fear of both success and failure wrap chains around me. And I am the only one who has done this to me.

I think the message I'm supposed to be getting here, is to stop letting the fear of drowning keep you from getting on the boat. I don't know where this boat will take me. But I suppose if Jesus can calm the seas and walk on water, He can steer the course of any boat that comes my way and say, "Get in." And maybe I will fall on my face, but how will I know, if I don't get on the boat?

It's like that joke about the man stranded on the island. A boat comes along, and he turns it down, saying, "No, God will save me." Two more boats come and he says the same thing to each of them. Then he cries out to God, "Why won't you save me?" God says, "I sent you three boats! What more do you want?"

Get on the boat. Go for the ride and see where it takes you. I think that's exactly what I'll do.

I Believe I Can Fly.... Maybe

Wouldn't it be cool to be able to fly? (And wouldn't it be cool to be able to work without ever leaving your house, but get paid enough to never have to worry about money? Oh, the dreams we have.)

When I was a young girl, I dreamed that I could fly. I could just lift off the ground and float through the air. I have no idea what that means, but I always loved that dream. I never felt so free and alive. This is fascinating to me and to people who know me, because I have always been afraid of heights.

I'm nervous on ladders. I am a very nervous flyer. I hold on for dear life during takeoffs and landings. I want to get up the courage to ride the Danny Phantom rollercoaster at Kings Island, which looks like the closest thing to flying I could ever get.

I read one of my daughter's books recently, called "Growing Wings." It's a coming-of-age book about a young girl who is actually growing wings. Wouldn't that be cool, to have real wings? I would definitely have to get over my fear of heights. In the book, the girl's back itched and ached with the growing of her wings. I feel as though I am still growing my wings some days. Metaphorically, of course.

While we grow up, lots of changes happen, and new things and people come and go. It can be scary, a bit like growing wings. I still get nervous and scared about new and different things. My job has now changed three times, each time bringing new changes and challenges. Some days, I really wish my wings were fully formed. In new jobs or other situations, it can be uncomfortable. You can almost ache in anticipation and itch to get out of certain situations.

I have a theory. I believe that my flying dreams are like a message, to not be afraid. What could life be like if you weren't afraid of failing, or falling? But, if you believe you can fly... imagine what you could accomplish... what you could achieve... what you could aspire to be. We put more limitations on ourselves, with fear, than anyone else could ever place on us.

If you can dream it, you can achieve it. I have never believed I could achieve anything. Perhaps that's what the dream is about. I hope to have that dream again soon, to encourage me. (But, just in case, if you find a job that doesn't require me to leave the house, let me know.)

My Son, the Preacher Man

My son is a pretty cool kid, if I do say so myself. He is going to be eight, and is the smartest kid I know. Don't get me wrong here; my girls are pretty spectacular themselves. They are all honor roll kids.

There is just something about him that makes him special. He shines. I am pretty sure I know why: He loves Jesus and he doesn't mind telling you about it. He also likes to inform me that even though he loves me a lot, he loves Jesus and God best. He drew a picture of the Last Supper for me once, and told me the story.

My grandmother says my son is the next Billy Graham, and he may very well be. At seven, he has more faith than a lot of adults I know. When my grandfather had a stroke and was very ill in the hospital, my grandmother was distraught. My son, listening to our conversation, interrupted us to tell her, "You don't need to worry about grandpa. God is with him and he doesn't worry about being alone. He is with you too!" Grandpa eventually went to be with Jesus.

He always makes sure we say our mealtime prayer, no matter where we are. One year at Christmas at my grandmother's house, everyone was getting their food and he said to my grandma, "Isn't anyone going to bless this food?" So my aunt said a prayer so everyone could eat.

One day, he was drawing pictures and he drew a picture with two paths. One led to a sign that said Go and another that said Stop.

He said to me, "Mommy, do you know how to get to heaven?"

I said, "Yes, but why don't you tell me anyway."

He said, "Look at my picture, there are two paths. One leads to the sign that says go, the other leads to a sign that says stop."

I said, "Yes, I see that."

He said, pointing at the Go path, "Well mom, if you take this path here, you believe in Jesus and you get to go to heaven."

I said, "OK..."

He said, "If you take this other path, you don't believe in Jesus and you have to stop. And you don't get to go to heaven. Do you know where you go?"

I said, "Tell me."

He said, "Well, you don't go to heaven, I can tell you that."

Once, when I was out of the house and my husband was home with the children, my son was playing an interactive Bible game on the TV. He went into the kitchen and asked for a piece of bread.

My husband said, "Sure. Do you want some butter or peanut butter on it?"

He said, "No, just the bread."

So my husband got it for him, and then my son asked, "Could I have some wine... or no, sorry, juice?"

My husband looked into the fridge and said, "We have orange juice, or Hawaiian Punch."

My son said, "OK, Hawaiian Punch will work." He proceeded to hold the bread and juice, one in each hand, then look down and pray, and take his version of communion in our kitchen.

When I tuck him in at night, we read. First, he picks a book he wants me to read to him, and then we read from a Bible. I say a Bible, because we have gone through several children's Bibles.

At night, he also says his prayers. Saying his prayers has been something he has done since he was able to speak. Before that, I said them for him. Before I leave his room at night, I always say, "God bless you and keep you safe through the night. I love you, my son, sleep well."

Recently he responded with, "May God be with you."

To which I respond, "...and also with you."

If that weren't enough, last night he followed that with, "May the warm winds of heaven blow across from your spirit." I did a double take.

When he grows up, he wants to be a world-traveling scientist. I think that it's a good possibility. For now, he is my missionary. He doesn't have to travel to spread the word of God. He need not look any further than his own house, with the older people who get hardened by life and beaten down by circumstances.

My son isn't the best on any sports team, although he loves to play. He doesn't wrestle, he rarely gets dirty, and he takes school seriously. But he will ask you to pull his finger, then burp or fart. He blows bubbles in his drink, and he sets things on the stairs instead of putting them away. He isn't perfect, and he's a typical boy in many ways. But my son loves Jesus. He loves me almost as much. That makes me happy. I tell people that he is like the sunshine among the storm clouds; he pulls us all together. God has great plans for him. I can't wait to see what they are.

If only everyone could have his faith. Keep shining that light son, keep shining that light, so that the entire world will see HIM through you.

The Man with The Cross

Tuesday turned out to be what my oldest child described as the weirdest day ever.

It all started with the car ride to the mall. It takes about twenty-five minutes to get there, so we have plenty of time to sing along with the radio, or sing whatever happens to pop into our heads at the time. For me, it was the "iCarly" theme song. For my daughter, it was "The Facts of Life" theme song; we were singing them at the same time in the car.

My daughter looked over at me, I glanced at her, and she said, "Really mom? You are singing iCarly?"

To which I respond something to the effect of, "Well I don't think iCarly is as great as 'The Facts of Life,' but you have to admit, her song is catchy." But it was a bit odd that I would be singing a song from her generation, and she one from mine.

The trip to the mall was uneventful. Although we did have a controversial discussion as to why we would not be eating our lunch in the Target snack shop. The town we live closest to doesn't have a lot of variety in terms of restaurants. To be fair, we don't have a Target, but I didn't drive a half hour to eat in a snack shop. I didn't drive a half an hour to eat at Taco Bell either, but to avoid further argument, I gave in. (This goes against everything I was taught as a child. My mother had a rule that when we went someplace with more restaurant choices, you could not eat at a place you had back home. A rule I strongly support and try to live by.)

We were driving back to the mall to pick up a book when we saw a man carrying a cross, walking down the side of the highway. This was not a small cross; this was a huge cross that he carried over his shoulder. This was very much a "if anyone would come after me, he must deny himself and take up his cross daily and follow me" (Luke 9:23) kind of cross. We looked and we looked again, and looked again. All the kids could say was, "Wow."

I said, "Well … that gives new meaning to it, don't you think?"

We had never seen anything like it. I have often wondered where he was going, and how often he got stopped on his journey, what he said when he was asked what he was doing. I wonder if he was asked to do it, or if he volunteered. And, I wonder how far he walked.

I'm not sure if the load he was carrying was more figurative or physical. I only know that since that day, I have wondered how heavy a cross each of us would have to carry, if all of our burdens were represented by one. If some of us would have crosses that would be so weighed down, we wouldn't be able to walk an inch, much less down an entire highway. I have even thought that maybe no one else noticed it that day, in their daily rush. I am only certain that I saw it because my children saw it too. In this day and age, it could have been a mirage. The sight of the man carrying the cross alongside the highway is one I won't soon forget.

What would you have thought, had you seen the man with the cross that day? Would you take up your cross and follow Him? What did he know that I didn't; what journey of discovery he was on that led him to that point? I suppose it's not for me to know. All I know is this: I don't know where he was going, and I know not his load.

I have been reading my *One Year Bible* and my *Daily Guidepost* this year. I pray and long to do His will every day in everything I do. Even if it's something I don't like to do. Even when I'm doing everyone's laundry or mopping the floor, I tell myself that I am not doing it for those who won't help clean; I'm doing it for God. Because this is what I've been called to do. Then I feel better, remembering that I'm in the exact place that I'm supposed to be, in this time of my life.

When my house is particularly messy and I'm the only one to clean it, I like to put on my tiara when I clean. That way, while I'm grumbling about what a hot mess it is, I can remember that even Cinderella had to clean up after people, and she was a princess.

From Competition to the Finish Line

I'm not sure I have a competitive bone in my body. I tend to clap for both teams of a sporting event when a good play happens. Although I want my children to succeed, I'm not sure it's best for them to always win, as I think the learning happens in the losing.

As a child, I was not athletic in any way, shape, or form. This has carried over into adulthood. I'm a klutz, simple as that. I cannot count the number of times I've fallen down the stairs, I can't run from my driveway to the stop sign a hundred yards away without thinking that the end of my life is near.

When I walk briskly, I try not to trip over a pebble, or my own two feet.

I did have dance training for seven years. You would think that this would have made me more graceful. Unfortunately, the only thing I got out of it is the ability to stand with my feet in first position. First position is not really a useful thing to know. What it amounts to is my tendency to walk like a duck. So no, I'm not an athlete.

I can think of no instance where I tend to get competitive unless it's playing Scrabble. As any mistake on my part will lead to years of ridicule, and me waiting for ten years for my husband to say or do something stupid so I can tease him back. I don't like to play cards. I don't have an attention span for half the board games we own.

In what other ways do we tend to compete? In this world of the haves and have-nots, do you compete, or do you simply relish in other' people's successes, and count the blessings that God has given you?

As a child, I had a friend who always seemed to need to one-up me. This bothered me at the time because I couldn't understand the need she had to be better than me all the time.

As I came from a dysfunctional family, I was given material things to make it better. As a kid, of course, you like the stuff and gladly accept it, even though what you really long for is the love and acceptance you will never gain. Perhaps I gave up any desire for competition, because the only things I ever wanted, I thought I would never get.

So when I got a TV for Christmas, my friend would get a TV and VCR. If I got a Commodore VIC20 computer, she'd get the equivalent of a Mac. I didn't grow up with Nike, I never met Ralph Lauren. I thought I lived in a house, only to grow up and discover I lived in a double-wide. But I could take you through my room and tell you who gave me each thing I ever owned. I was thankful. Perhaps that's the difference today with children, and some adults. Those who have grown up always having take for granted what they have, and don't know what they have been fortunate enough not to have had to deal with. Those who had nothing, but grew up to have their dreams come true, understand the gift of being grateful.

I don't have to know the reasons for everything, I don't have to understand why I didn't grow up like "The Brady Bunch." I can tell you this, though: to feel the sunshine, feel the breeze and know the joy that unfolds when you walk in the light… there is nothing greater. I have felt the presence of God in my house. I have seen His miracles in my life.

I'm a sinner. I am a work in progress. I am the farthest thing from perfect you will ever see. Do I still mess up daily? Yes, but you don't walk into a college class and immediately know everything after the first session. It takes time and effort, along with a willingness to admit your faults. He already knows them all anyway. You may as well confess them and save some time. I also have to believe He has a sense of humor, otherwise, what on earth would He want with me?

There are people in this world who need to blame others for the bad things that happen in the world. The target is usually God. "Why does God not put an end to my pain?" they ask. I have a question: Did you ask Him to?

"Why doesn't He stop bad things from happening?" Free will. He wants you to come to Him. He wants you help you, because He loves you beyond anything you can even comprehend.

I'm not a preacher. I couldn't lead a Sunday school class of two-year-olds. The amount I don't know far surpasses what I do know. You don't have to listen to me. You can say, "That lady has lost her mind." But let me ask you this: What if there is a reason I'm so happy and actually grew the courage up to type all this out for the world to see?

Those who know me know I like to write, but I tend not to lean to anything very serious. So call this my medium. Of course, it's all still being written. But I can tell you where I've been and how I got out of the pit. It surely wasn't anything I did. But my God is mighty.

Entitled

I am troubled. As I was trying to nap, my mind just kept swimming with how sad I am by a certain group of people. Perhaps you know them. There is an entire generation of them; it probably spans several generations in families. It's the people with a sense of entitlement. They just really believe that the world owes them. They should be given whatever they want. These people worry me. You might even say I am fearful of them. (We are often fearful of things we do not understand.)

To those people I would like to say, "Who are you, that you believe that your existence is somehow more important than others'? What have you done for the world that the world should owe you anything?"

Perhaps the better question is: "What wrong has been bestowed upon you that you feel you now deserve something spectacular as a prize? Are you a knight from the round table? Or have you just fallen on hard times and you see no other way out?"

John 16:33 tells us, "I have told you these things, so that in me you may have peace. In this world you will have trouble. But take heart! I have overcome the world."

I am not a quick learner. I need to be hit over the head with something until I understand it. God is so patient with me. I am not always a patient person. I used to pray for patience. I now know that if you pray for patience, God just gives you opportunities to be patient. He then uses these opportunities to grow us and develop us into who we are meant to be. I no longer pray for patience. I pray for Him to soften my heart towards those who may frustrate me.

God created the universe with himself at the center, not you. He even left us with an instruction manual for our life. It's called the Bible. I do not have it memorized, which is why I keep a copy in several locations in my house so I can refer to it at will. I know that anything I need to know I can just look up. (If I can remember what the verse says, but not the address, I can Google it and it tells me where to find it.)

From the outside looking in, my life to someone else might look perfect. I will admit that I have been blessed, by no fault of my own. I do not deserve it. My life as it stands now is solely by the grace of God. I spent a few years in the pit of depression. Those years were trying and nothing that I would wish upon my worst enemy. And yet, I find now that I am so thankful for them. Through them, God has grown me. Those years were as an adult. I will not get into the troubles and suffering endured as a child. I will only say that even with all of the bad things that happened, I never felt like I was owed anything because of it. Perhaps it was my upbringing.

Are you a "Why me?" whiner kind of person? If so, I would ask you, "Why not you?" Are you paying attention to what you are being taught? Welcome to the human race. You will have trouble. You are not above it. You cannot escape it. (John 16:33 says, "In this world we will have trouble.") It's kind of a DUH moment, isn't it? The point I am attempting to make here, is that everyone has trouble. You are not special because of *your* trouble. You can spend your entire life trying to figure out 'why you,' or you can get over yourself, and say, "What can I learn from this?"

I spent a long time grieving the loss of my mother. A few short years after I lost her, I miscarried our fourth child, and the day after I was told my baby was not to be, the only grandfather I ever knew died. That was the second time I found my way into a pit. But it didn't last as long. (I seem to learn quicker as I go along.)

At that point, God just spoke to me, and said something to the effect of, "Really? Do we need to go here again? Or are you going to listen to Me now?" I moved pretty quickly after that. It's not a place I want to return to. If you read the rest of the verse in John 16:33, God tells us, "Take Heart! I have overcome the world." So what you can take away from my experience is this: This is not our home. God has overcome this world and we will someday leave this place and move on to where He is. So don't wallow in self-pity or get caught up in sadness.

I guess that is why I don't mourn for my mother as much as I once did. Sure, I miss her. There are things I wish she were here to experience with us. Mostly though, I think I am a bit

jealous. She has completed this journey. She has moved on for good, and her times of trouble are over. She saw God conquer the world and she is now with Him. Who am I to not want that for her?

I am but a speck of dust blowing in the wind; someday I will float away from here and see her again. When I go, the light will be on, and she will be waiting. I will also meet the child that went before me. Oh, what a day that will be.

Grace

I am a work in progress, as many who know me will attest to. I am proud, opinionated, strong-willed, self-centered, and set in my ways. I have great expectations of others. I cannot watch a high school, college, or professional sporting event without getting upset if they miss a point. Professional sports are the worst, because they are getting paid big money just to play a game—shouldn't they be perfect?

I understand my own limitations. I just fall short when it comes to understanding others. This is especially true with the people I love most, my children. I tend to forget that they are still learning. That they haven't been here on this planet as long as I have, and while they should (at the ages they are now) know what is expected of them, I should know better than to expect perfection of them, when I myself fall short every single day.

Before I had children, I had several theories as to the best way to raise a child. One of those was that they should fear you. My mother had a "look" that was a gauge to tell me how quickly she would blow her stack. I envision my face turning different colors of red when my children are being rotten. I think they should know when that red reaches a certain shade, they should start backpedaling. They do not.

Apparently, I do not in fact turn different shades of red; I just look like the bride of Frankenstein, and they laugh rather than run. They take me to the edge and then leap. It's not like I don't follow through on my threats. While I have never beaten my children, when they were younger and easier to catch, they did get a spanking on occasion. Now, if you want to hit them where it hurts, you take their electronics away.

In my growing, I sometimes have to be hit over the head over and over again before I get it. The thing I could never figure out about God is this: Why on earth would He want me? I fall short every day. I argue with my children, and I yell at them about things, which I swore I would never do (my mother was the queen of yelling). And yet here I am, a yelling mom. It makes me distraught. And, I compare myself to others. I have heard the root of all evil is money. I would have to disagree; I think comparing oneself to others is.

I have said that the neighborhood was great until all the "perfect" people moved in. What makes them so perfect to me? Their yards are well manicured. Their houses are always clean when I walk in. How do they do it? I can barely keep up with the laundry. (Oh, who am I kidding? I can't keep up with the laundry at all.) There is always a pile of papers or stuff waiting to be put away. And somehow, it's a big surprise every night that we need to go to bed.

What on earth could God use me for? I'm still not sure. But as I learn more about grace, I know He does want me, and that it's not just me that falls short. Everyone does. Everyone sins. In my self-centeredness, I truly believed it was just me. I can't even keep up with the neighbors; how on earth am I to measure up to be a child of God? But thankfully, I don't have to. I have to keep reminding myself that God has given us grace. His love is so great and so far reaching that even me, the least of these, is covered by his love and grace. Imagine that, even me!

A Letter to Heaven

I went to the movies with a group of friends to see "Joyful Noise." If you haven't had the pleasure of seeing this movie, I would highly recommend it. I cannot imagine who wouldn't enjoy a movie with both Dolly Parton and Queen Latifah in it. The music was really good. And it was funny.

When I arrived home, my family was in bed. I set my things down and went to the kitchen to clear the table, when I noticed an envelope addressed to "Heaven," in my son's crayon handwriting. The return address said "Me." Where the stamp would go was a smiley face. While this shouldn't surprise me, it isn't every day you come home and find a letter addressed to Heaven on your table.

My son is a kindhearted, loving, warm, open, sensitive child. I call him my little peacekeeper. He hates conflict of any kind. He has this faith that is pure. He openly believes. He says his prayers. He talks to his friends about God. He has talks with his sisters that lead me to believe when he is a father himself, his wife and children will be lucky to have him.

Later, he asked if I saw his letter. I told him that I did, and I asked him what it said. He just shook his head and didn't want to tell me. I asked him if he requested different parents. He said no. I asked him if he wanted different sisters. He said no, although it was tempting. He wants me to mail it on my way to work. It is taking a great deal of restraint on my part not to open it.

How does one go about mailing a letter to Heaven? Has anyone else ever encountered this situation? What's the protocol here? God already knows what the letter says, I'm sure. He knows my son's heart. But there is something about this letter. I'm not sure if I should open it or not. As his mother, I want to see him happy. I want to know what he struggles with, what his hopes are, what he dreams about.

Do I read it so I can pray for the things he is asking for along with him? Do I not open it and just keep it in my Bible? My boy is nine but I'm not sure he fully understands the postal system. If I took it to the post office, would the postmaster just throw it away? Would the postmaster open it and read it?

Have you ever written actual letters to Heaven? My letters are more conversations with a Father. He is my guidance counselor, He is my therapist, He is my parent, He is my everything. A prayer is free, no postage necessary. It's a toll-free call, as they used to say. You can call any time, day or night. God also has many houses and you can visit the closest one to you.

I am curious to see what God is planning for my son. I can't wait to see what God uses him for. Mostly though, I love to watch him explore the world. I like to watch his mind work. Maybe he will be a pastor, or a missionary, or a doctor, or a teacher. He could become anything at all. But for now, I love that he is just a little boy who is good at being a little boy, and he loves Jesus and loves his mom and dad, and, most of the time, his sisters.

Keeping it Real....Serious

Smiling Through the Tears

When you've been to as many funerals as I have, you have to have a sense of humor. It sounds backwards, but it's the only way to get through it. Not that I haven't grieved, or have my bouts with sadness and discouragement. I just know that, for me, you have to find an opportunity to laugh or you go a bit crazy. We have an awesome God, who has to have a sense of humor; I know He gets my sense of humor.

July is always rough for me. July is the month that my mother passed away; the day before my birthday. This puts a monkey wrench in any thoughts of celebration. When I lost my mother, I fell into a pit of depression that lasted for about two years. I just couldn't believe that the only parent who I believed cared about me, was gone.

Now that I'm a healthier, livelier me, I think she figured that if she was going to go, she'd go in July to make sure I'd always remember her on my birthday. The first couple of years I spent hiding, or rather running away, from any and all reminders of her. Now, it's just something that is a part of my birth month and I accept it—still begrudgingly.

I try to remind myself of how we used to fight. Whenever my oldest starts arguing with me and driving me crazy, I call her by my mother's name, which in turn makes her crazy.

This month, however, we lost my cousin over the Fourth of July weekend. She had been very ill with cancer for a long time. In fact, when she was a baby, they didn't give her but two years to live. She lived 36 years. She always had a smile, she never complained, and every single time I saw her, she had a hug for me and told me she loved me. If only we could all live by that example.

I cannot imagine what my aunt and uncle are going through. They have now lost both of their children, having lost their oldest a couple of years ago to a tragic accident. Seeing their look of complete defeat—even as my aunt said they were praising God that she was now with Him in heaven—completely broke my heart.

After the viewing, as I lay in bed, I wept for them. I also wept for me, because I felt so helpless to help them, because I'd had no magic words to share. I fumbled along, saying practically nothing. What do you say to a broken man that says to you, "I just wish we could have had her a while longer, you know?"

What do you say to the heartbroken woman that says to you, "I can't lose my mom now, I'll never get through this if she dies, too." I begged God to get us through this time and to keep me upright, at least for them.

The next morning was my cousin's funeral, and we all gathered to pay our respects. There were three preachers that spoke. It was really just a perfect service. Afterwards, we all gathered in the atrium and talked. It was cold in the building, so when they released us to go to our cars, everyone gladly went outside to get warm in their cars.

Grandma had been in the atrium with us, but apparently no one told her to go to a car. So we're all sitting in our cars waiting for the procession to begin, while my uncle, who had brought Grandma, comes walking through the line of cars throwing his hands in the air, yelling, "I can't find my mom!"

I found this funny. A grown man walking through stopped traffic, trying to find his mom. Then my cousin's wife came to our car window, to see if we'd stolen Grandma. Once we stopped giggling, we decide go look for Grandma.

We all got out of our cars, checked the church's restrooms and the lounge. The entire time I kept thinking, she is probably on the other side of the building. As I walked back outside to go to my car, here came Grandma, being walked around the building by the Schwann's delivery man, who happens to be a friend of the family. They hurriedly put her in a car and the procession went ahead to the cemetery.

Once we were out of the car, she said to me, "It's the darndest thing. I just walk outside to get warm, and all of YOU get lost."

All of us got lost; what a perspective. I think all of us do get lost, at times. I think, in the hustle and bustle of life, we just get turned around from what is really important. I will miss my cousin, just as I miss my mother every day. But it's good to know, that even in the midst of tears, with God, you can always find a reason to smile.

My Mother: A Story of Getting to the Other Side

There was a lightning storm the night she went to be with Jesus.

The day had been hot, sunny, and bright. The pool was used, and the laughter I heard that day from inside was wonderful. I was tired. I was tired a lot in those days. I got the baby down for a nap, and after a quick peek into her room to check on her, I laid down on the couch for a nap.

Then I heard the sliding glass door open. I felt a hand on my arm to wake me. I awoke and looked into some sad eyes, and knew that rest would not come easily for a long time.

The children were sent home with Grandma, and phone calls were made. Someone brought a meal to the house. I didn't need to be convinced to eat, though; food was my comfort. Eating was easy. It was the rest that was hard. My husband tried to comfort me, while feeling helpless at the same time.

Mom had been living with us, though she spent most of her time in a hospital bed in a spare room. So at least we didn't have to travel. Mom's best friend came to the house, and the night wore on. I finally told my uncle to go home, and my husband to get some sleep. But one look at mom's best friend told me she wasn't going anywhere. I on one side of the bed and her on the other, we kept our vigil.

I have always been afraid of storms. Yet on this night, I couldn't keep from looking out the window, behind the head of her bed, where a lightning show played outside. She never woke up, but we could tell a war was going on inside. One look at her and you would see that though she was standing firm, she was losing her battle. Somehow, she wasn't ready to go. She wasn't going to go, I thought. Yet, there she was… going.

I spent my time praying. Talking to her and telling her what I thought she needed to hear. I don't know if she heard any of my words. I told her that she had done her job. And that I would be OK. My husband and our children would be there for me. My mother-in-law had promised she would take care of me, too. It's OK to go, I told her. I knew she would be better; the pain and suffering would end. Then I told her I loved her, and that God would make it OK.

I'm not sure how I knew, other than feeling an overwhelming sense of presence. But suddenly, I knew it was time. "Take her hand," I told her friend. She looked at me, and I said, "It's time. She's leaving." I looked for Him, because I could feel Him, like He stood at the end of the bed, but now I think I felt more than I saw. Then mom seemed to get up and walk from her body and into His arms. She was gone… forever.

Then I went upstairs and told my husband she was gone. My house, which had been full of people coming and going, would fill up only a couple more times. Then this journey, that had begun the summer before, would be coming to an end.

The diagnosis of lung cancer was not the worst of it; it had already spread and was in her brain by the time they saw it. They only gave her six to eight months. "I hope to give her a good season," the doctor said. Had it really been almost a full year?

She was to wear white, "because angels wear white, and that is what she is now," I said. I wore a yellow sweater because it was her favorite color.

After the funeral, I walked into her room and collapsed.

Surrounded by funeral flowers, I wept. That was the beginning of the darkness. The darkness would embrace me into its folds and hold me tight for some time. I would go through the motions of living, without really living. I would be numb. I would refuse to feel. There would be entire days when I would simply sit and not do anything at all. I wouldn't get dressed; I wouldn't clean the house; I wouldn't shower. I would only exist.

I spent my time blaming myself, God, and the doctors for her death. It seemed all had been incompetent—unable to do what I thought to be a simple thing... save her. Mostly, I blamed myself.

The accusing voices rang in my ears, telling me what I felt I already knew to be truth: I had done this; I had given up; I had let her die! It had been my job to save her, and I failed. She had asked me only to fight and not give up. What had I done?

Instead of holding onto the God who had come to take her home and make her well again, the One who had given me peace that night that He was here, I ran away from Him and hid. Again, the accusing voices rang in my head: "Unworthy. Helpless. Worthless." Inside this overwhelming sense of failure, I also felt that I didn't belong in His arms, and was deserving of the hell I had placed upon myself.

It would be at least two years before the sun would shine in my heart again. If you were to ask my mother-in-law about that time in my life, she would tell you that she thought they had lost me, too. I believe they did for a while. Only through God's grace did I make my way back. Only God could save me and take the burden from me. At this point, I can't remember how He pulled me out of it and brought me out. I do know that I did slip back into despair briefly one other time since. But He pulled me out before I got too far in again.

I know now that the only way I can get through this life is to hold onto Him with all my might and not let go. God loves me, and if I fall, He will pick me back up again.

I'm not finished learning the lessons from that painful journey. Perhaps someone else can learn from mine, like how not to get through a tragedy. Nevertheless, I've grown. Not all the way to where I'm intended to go, as I fight daily with my fears. It's only now, almost seven years later, that I am able to live in my house without sadness. I know He has a plan, and I'm happy to be along for the ride — even on the bumpiest roads.

A Birthday, an Ugly Cake, and Breaking Free

Friday, February 25. It seems like a day that would be like any other day, and yet this year it was different. The kids were out of school because of snow, my hubby had the day off, and it would have been my mother's 59th birthday.

In the years since she passed, that day has been a source of great sadness for me. In our family, birthdays were a big deal. Parties and gifts were given, and time with family was truly the icing on the cake.

Then there was the actual cake. My mother made the most beautiful cakes you can imagine. She always made my birthday cakes, and when I had my children, she made their cakes. When it came time for her birthday, I decided one year that she should have a cake, too, and that I would bake one. Her favorite cake was a banana cake with peanut butter icing. If you have gone to your local grocery store to look for a box mix for a banana cake with peanut butter icing, you will not find it, as I found out the hard way. So I made a banana cake from scratch, along with homemade peanut butter icing that my mother had to instruct me over the phone how to make.

In the years since her passing, I have been up and down. I got so wrapped up in what I had lost, I didn't take time to look at anything that I still had. I forgot to look up; I forgot to look outside of myself. The thing with depression is this: you are content with just hurting yourself. I have said that so many times that it breaks my heart. What you forget is that in hurting yourself, you also hurt the ones that love you.

This year, I shed only a single tear for my mother. I didn't spend my day in mourning for someone who is walking the Streets of Gold. Instead, I baked a banana cake from scratch, with peanut butter icing. The cake didn't rise and may have been the ugliest cake ever baked. However, as with God's love, icing covered the cake, making it good, just as God's love covered the ugliness of my pit while pulling me out. We said happy birthday to Grandma this year, while celebrating her life. We talked about our memories of her, while enjoying a not-perfect cake, but it a cake made out of love and hope.

This year, I am determined to read through my entire One Year Bible that I started when mom was sick. This year I am finally doing the Bible study that my best friend said would change my life. I'm memorizing a verse from the Bible, which I think it says it all:

Isaiah 61:1-4.
The Spirit of the Sovereign LORD is on me, Because the LORD has anointed me to preach good news to the poor. He has sent me to bind up the brokenhearted, to proclaim freedom for the captives and release from darkness for the prisoners, to proclaim the year of the LORD's favor and the day of vengeance of our God, to comfort all who mourn, and provide for those who grieve in Zion — to bestow on them a crown of beauty instead of ashes, the oil of gladness instead of mourning, and a garment of praise instead of a spirit of despair. They will be called oaks of righteousness, a planting of the LORD for the display of his splendor. They will rebuild the ancient ruins and restore the places long devastated; they will renew the ruined cities that have been devastated for generations.

To fully get out of my pit, I needed to break free from the chains that bound me. I don't want to have a spirit of mourning. Is that living? Is that becoming who God has chosen me to be? So I will praise Him and seek Him and not despair. After all, my mother couldn't be in better hands.

Conversations Only a Mother Could Love

Daphne: Mom, why do they call it a purse?

Me: I don't know.

Daphne: Well, it doesn't purr at you.

Scotty: Yeah, and it doesn't ssss like a snake!

Me: I don't know.

Daphne: Well, Why don't they call it a hand bag?

Me: Some people do.

Daphne: Then why call it a purse?

Me: I don't know. Some people call it a shoulder bag.

Daphne: Then why call it a purse?

Me: I DON'T KNOW!

Daphne: And what's the deal with the man bag?

Me: Only Joey from "Friends" had one of those.

Daphne: But it was like a purse, they said so... so why do they call it a purse?

Me: I don't know. Google it!

Daphne: Hey mom, did you know that Monique Coleman is older than Britney Spears?

Me: Remind me who Monique Coleman is?

Daphne: Uh, hello? "High School Musical"?

Me: Oh, right.

Daphne: Yeah, she's like 28. Can you believe that?

Me: It's nice when you look younger than you are. For example, I don't look a day over 32.

Daphne: Yeah right! Try a day over 52, maybe!

Me: This is why I sing in the car.

Me: Sit down and let me trim your bangs before I do your hair for school.

Daphne: OK.

(After finishing trim and while drying hair) Me: Wow, I did a really good job. Maybe I could be a professional bangs trimmer when I grow up.

Daphne: Uh yeah, deadline for going to beauty school, is age 30. Oops … sorry, ya missed it!

Me: Oh come on, really?

Daphne: Mom, I'd rather you just stayed home.

Me: Well, I won't be home today. So there!

Daphne: Really? Where ya goin'?

Me: Well, I'm cleaning the house.

Daphne: You have to leave for that?

Me: No. But I'll leave after. You know, if you kids would clean up after yourselves, I would get to leave earlier.

Daphne: Yeah? Well, that's why you're the favorite.

(Moral of the story: I still can't get any props around here.)

Sunday night conversation:

Vaughn: Did you set the alarm?

Me: No, why? I don't have school in the morning.

Vaughn: So you are not getting up with the kids?

Me: I don't need an alarm to get up with the kids. Even if you get up, the kids always come in and make sure I know they're up, thereby waking me up and ruining my sleep pattern.

Vaughn: Didn't you say you aren't sleeping well anyway?

Me: Well sure, but I like deciding when I'm done. It's kind of like when you use public toilets that flush by themselves.

Vaughn: You don't like public toilets?

Me: Well, no. Sometimes you are just doing your business and the thing flushes on its own. I always think, "How do you know I'm done? I'll let you know when I'm done." What kind of technology is that, anyway? Is it a motion detector? Is it Pee Pee Technology?

Vaughn: You are considerably faster when using a public restroom than you are at home.

Me: That's because half the time at home, I'm just hiding.

Vaughn: OK, can we go to sleep now?

Me: Sure, knock yourself out.

While at a volleyball game:

Daphne: Dude! Guess what I just figured out?

Me: What?

Daphne: By the time Scotty graduates, you will totally be pushing 50!

Me: Really? Was that necessary?

Daphne: Yeah, like, people will say, "Hey, is that your grandma?" And he will have to say, "No, that's my mom."

Me: I'll have you know I haven't aged a day in the last 10 years.

Daphne: Really, mom? Really?

(At which point, I relocate to a different seat. Sometimes it's hard to be me.)

Daphne: Hey mom, I brought home some information about class rings.

Me: Class rings for what?

Daphne: Uh, hello? High school, class rings, you know you have one, has the year you graduated on it? Anything?

Me: Yes, I understand the concept. It's the reason you are ready for one that I'm having a bit of trouble understanding.

Daphne: Mom, I'm in high school. That's when you wear a class ring.

Me: Yes, but how do I know you will graduate on time? Perhaps we should wait a couple years to make sure.

Daphne: Really, mom? Really? I'm an A/B student, you're gonna question my graduating on time?

Me: Well, perhaps you will have trouble with Trig.

Daphne: What's that?

Me: Point made! Score 1 for mom! <begins dancing>

Daphne: Perhaps we could discuss this after you have some time to process.

Me: Oh, I've processed. It's gonna take a little bit more than that. I'm thinking medication. I'm thinking therapy. I'm also thinking I should have a mother's ring before you are too old to be included on it.

Daphne: So when I graduate you will have me removed?

Me: No, but perhaps you will still consider yourself a child a little longer if I get one of those first.

Daphne: You need help! I'm going upstairs.

Me: <hits emergency chocolate supply and settles in with a book with vampires and other things that make sense>

Scotty: Mommy, who is your favorite child?

Me: I love all my kids the same.

Scotty: Oh, come on mom, you know you love me best.

Me: Sshh! Don't tell your sisters!

Scotty: Hey mom? Do you know the difference between heaven and you know, the other place?

Me: Well, yes, but do you?

Scotty: Well, I know that if you don't believe in Jesus, you are going to be praying you don't go to the other place!

Scotty: So all mammals give milk, right?

Vaughn: Yes.

Scotty: OK, so are coconuts mammals then? Cause they give milk.

Vaughn: No, they are a fruit.

Scotty: But you said that mammals give milk and coconuts are hairy like mammals.

Vaughn: Yes, they are, but they don't have spines, so they aren't mammals.

Scotty: So you are telling me this hairy thing that gives milk isn't a mammal?

Vaughn: Yes, that is what I'm telling you.

Scotty: Well, I'm staying away from it!

Scotty: Hey Mom! If you could have a super power, what would it be?

Me: I would want the ability to fly.

Scotty: That's what I thought you'd say. Do you wish you had a flying car?

Me: Sometimes. It would definitely be easier to parallel park. I could just float into a parking space. Also, it might alleviate the need to go backward, because my flying car could turn on a dime.

I brought my grandma by the house to show some of the remodeling projects. My cats happened to be standing at the door when we were ready to leave. She says to me, "Oh my! You have two cats?"

I said, "Yes grandma, for about 10 years now."

She says, "That lady next door to me has 3 cats and another lady I know had 2 dogs, and do you know what? They keep them in the house and let them sleep with them." She continues, "You don't let yours in the house, do you?"

I say, "They come in occasionally, but they don't stay in long, then they go back out."

She says, "Well, let me tell you something, if I ever get so lonely I need a cat or dog to come sleep with me, you put me in the nearest home! Because that's just sad!"

I love my granny.

Me: I'm having a hard day. I need you to give me some space. I've gotten bad news about some people and I need time to process.

Kid: Mom, I'm sorry, but I want you to know that you are loved. Us kids and dad all love you, so you aren't alone, OK?

Me: That's so sweet, thank you honey. I love all of you, too.

<Now flash forward about 30 minutes>

Me: Why don't you guys go outside and play? You could ride bikes, or take a walk or go swim.

Same kid who was just filled with love and understanding: UGH! Why can't you just leave us alone! We don't want to go outside!

Me: When I was a kid, there was no way we would have been allowed to sit around inside on such a nice day.

Kid: There was no "we," there was only "you," and no one was around to tell YOU anything.

Me: Well, I suppose that's true, BUT at least I was smart enough to go out and enjoy the day when it was nice. And why am I arguing with you, anyway? Get outside. I'm the mom; I did the labor, I fed you, I bathed you, I've kept you alive for the last 10 years, so do what I say and go swing on the swings!

(And with that, three kids pull away from electronics and go sit in a clubhouse to decide whose turn it is tomorrow to give me gray hair.)

If you could have any superhero power, what would it be?
Which superhero is the coolest: Batman, Superman, or Spiderman?
Which superhero that I made up do you like best?

Answers:

1. I would want to be the superhero you came up with called Ice Girl, because she can freeze anything, even time, and I could be with you longer.

2. Superman, because he can fly.

3. Spider Monkey Man, because he can climb like you.

Me: Hey grandma, want to go to lunch with me today?

Grandma: Oh no, honey. I'm not dressed to go out. Besides, I have a TV dinner out.

Me: Well, put it back in the freezer and let's go out. You're 84 years old; why do you care what people think of your outfit?

Grandma: No, no, I can't go. I already poked the holes in the TV dinner.

(Apparently once the holes are poked, it's a done deal.)

I Want to Grow Up, I Want to Grow Old, I Want to Grow Wings

In my most recent adult Bible study, I have been reading about believing, and believing in, God. As a child, I grew up going to church with friends, as my parents didn't go. A bus came around the neighborhood to pick up the kids and take them to church. I went to both Sunday school and the church service, and I always came home singing.

My mother was married to a man who was not my father. (I saw my biological father on birthdays and holidays, and on rare instances in between.) He also made it clear he didn't like children, and made our lives miserable for many years. I grew up hearing daily that I was ugly, I was worthless, and I would never amount to anything. He would ridicule and criticize my every move. Not having an ally, I believed every word. There were times that I would come home in high school and the lights wouldn't work, or I wouldn't be able to get in the house because my key wouldn't work.

But at church, I was uplifted, and told that there was a God, and he loved me. I believed in God always. I tried to be a good person. I was shy and scared most of the time, and although I believed IN God, I never quite *believed* Him. Someone could love me, just the way I was? Really? Because after all, who was I?

A song by Casting Crowns called "Who Am I" speaks to the heart of every fear I ever had. Growing up rejected, I was nobody, at home, or at school. I still have many fears and insecurities, but they are different ones than they used to be. Today, I know better. I am not a nobody, and I am loved. God loves me and He has given me the gift of a family.

I have a husband who is everything I could hope for, and three children. One kid is shy and quiet, who never learned to stick up for herself. The second one is a little more outgoing, and tries different things, but sometimes gets overlooked, which can make her very frustrated. The last one, my boy, is full of life, love, and compassion for others. When I am having trouble accepting change, I look at my son, who God put in my life to ground me. I've said before that he is my missionary. I love them all more than words could ever express, and I love God even more.

I have dreams of growing up, growing old, and growing wings. I am human, and I make mistakes along the way, which is why I need to grow up. I'm learning, and it's all I can do. I want to grow old, as so many in my family weren't so lucky. My own mother died at 52 from cancer. That's far too young. I'd like to see every one of my grandchildren born and grown. After all, what greater pleasure is there, than to see your children with their own children?

You may think I want to grow wings because I want to fly. I suppose that's partly true. I am a nervous flier, however. But I have something else in mind: I want to fly on the wings of angels. I want to see heaven and look into the face of God, and with tears streaming, thank Him for his rich blessings in my life. I want to be able to say that I did the best I could and that I accomplished what He sent me to do.

I have no earthly idea what the plan is. But I have every intention of giving my children the things I never had. Someone to stick up for them when they are unable to stick up for themselves. If there is another child in need, then I'll stick up for them too. Too many times, they go unnoticed. Too often, they need a voice outside of their own, and I'm not shy anymore.

I have some other things I'd like to do. I love my MOPS group so much, I refuse to leave it. I just keep going back and taking care of the little ones. It's good for the mothers to have a break, and it's good for me to rock a baby and remember how small they start out.

But they grow and they go to school, and when they get to about nine, it all starts changing. The tween and teen years are hard, which is why we need a MOTS (Mothers of Teenagers) group. It's hard when you've held them so long, to start letting them go. It's also important for the kids to know that you are still there for them. That even though they are

growing up, you aren't going to just walk away. And clingy parents (like me) need to learn to let them stand on their own, and be confident that they will make the right decisions.

Only when we support each other can we be confident that our legs will keep us standing. God calls us to love each other. If we do that, and truly believe that He is holding us all up, there is nothing we can't accomplish.

Roses Are Red (poems)

Still

In the stillness of the night that is where I find you,

In the gentle breeze through the trees you call to me,

In the softness of a whisper I hear your voice.

In the shadows of the trees I see you silhouetted with light.

In the flutter of a butterfly's wing my heart speeds up,

In the blooming of a daisy I call your name.

In the moment it takes to look up,

You are gone and the absence shatters forevermore.

The Stay-at-Home Mom Song

Oh give me a home,

Where a maid does so roam,

And the skies are not cloudy all day,

Where seldom is heard a discouraging word,

And the house stays clean every day.

Home, home in never, never land,

Where the dishes do themselves,

Where the meals are all free,

And the laundry all clean,

And you can relax and read books all day.

The Future

If I were to live to be 110,

I wonder about the changes to the world then.

Will the stars shine brighter?

Or will they be seen at all?

Will the sun still hang high in the sky?

Or would it be tired and pass us by?

But if I live to be just 103,

I'll remember the kindness you've shown to me.

And when I see the Son way up in the clouds,

I'll tell Him it was nice to have met you in the crowd.

I'll thank Him for the stars that twinkled up high,

I'll thank Him for the moon that shined so bright,

I'll thank Him for the grass so green,

I'll thank Him for the season of spring.

I'll thank Him for the dirt in the ground that grew the food that kept me around.

I'll thank Him for water so fresh and clean,

I'll thank Him for my loving family.

I'll thank Him for each day I was given,

For I know now that I'm forgiven.

***

Delight in the gifts God has given you,

Rejoice in the love that surrounds you,

Embrace your loved ones while you have them

And pray to one day be worthy to stand in HIS presence.

Remember the ONE who provides all things

to be thankful for.

God bless you all!

***

Acknowledgements

First and foremost, I want to thank God for this opportunity. I wouldn't be here without His guidance and grace.

Next, the most wonderful partner a woman could ever hope for, my husband "Vaughn" for his encouragement and love. You are my "ambassador of Kwan," man, and I love you!

My children, for allowing me to share their lives with the world. I love you "to infinity and beyond" — and all exactly the same.

My best friend Christi Morton for being the best counselor and cheerleader, even when I am exasperating.

My editor/publisher extraordinaire, Shannon Janeczek, for believing in this newbie and building me up when my fear threatened to take over. By extension, I also thank Theresa Cole and Katie Rokakis for helping out with polishing, formatting, and marketing my manuscript.

To Megan Dillingham for believing in me as well, and introducing me to Shannon.

My grandmother, Mary Lou Myers, for passing on her love of reading to me.

Thank you to Karen Nowosatko for fantastic cover art.

The other five people who knew about this project and kept it on the down-low till it was ready to be revealed — you know who you are.

About the Author

Heather Nestleroad was born in a small Midwestern town to parents who loved each other, until they didn't anymore. She then spent the rest of her childhood watching family shows and dreaming of one day having a family just like on TV. After getting married and having children, one day she discovered she did have a family like that, only funnier.

Heather now lives in yet another small Midwestern town with her husband, three children, and two cats. When she isn't writing about the hilarity in her own life, she is working with kindergarteners, going to Bible study, driving her children to various destinations, searching for the best place to have lunch, and looking for ways to get out of cooking dinner.

You can visit her at her blog: NestledinSuburbia.com.

www.ingramcontent.com/pod-product-compliance
Lightning Source LLC
Chambersburg PA
CBHW061640040426
42446CB00010B/1507